The
Message of
Exodus

The Message of Exodus

A Theological Commentary

Lester Meyer

AUGSBURG Publishing House • Minneapolis

To Joan

Contents

Preface

This commentary is intended for those who want to study the Book of Exodus. It is not an aid to devotion and meditation, though it has something to contribute to those commendable exercises. Neither is it a work of specialized, technical scholarship, though it builds on such works. No previous acquaintance with Exodus (or any other biblical book) is assumed. What *is* assumed is a willingness to struggle seriously with the text in order to grasp its meaning.

Because there is a great variety among biblical commentaries, it is appropriate at the outset to say something about the scope of this one. Its focus is not primarily on historical matters. Historical scholarship provides a valuable service by directing our attention to the origins and development of the various parts of the Bible, and their relation to the course of events. To analyze the Scriptures into their earlier components, and to relate these blocks and strands of material to the times about which they tell and to which they were addressed, is an important aspect of biblical studies. For the word of God is never an abstraction. It speaks of and in the concrete realities experienced by the people of God. Interesting and important as these historical matters may be, however, they are not the main concern of this commentary.

Neither is the focus primarily on literary matters. Literary scholarship also provides a valuable service in helping us to recognize the integrity and effectiveness of the Bible as literature, and the richly varied forms of expression which it contains. The application of this approach to the Book of Exodus has shown it to be a literary work of considerable sophistication, uniting narrative, genealogy, poetry, and law into an artistic whole which is able to move the reader as only a work of art can do. The insights of literary scholarship find a place in this commentary, but its first priority is not Exodus as literature.

It is, rather, religious matters that will concern us most. Certainly these cannot be treated in isolation from historical and literary considerations. But it was, after all, from *religious* motives that Israel, throughout its long history, recalled and reflected on the events of the story told here. And it was from *religious* motives that Israel shaped that story until it became the work of literature we now know. To view it as if it existed primarily to provide information about the past or artistic pleasure in the present would be to miss the point. The Book of Exodus puts every generation in touch with the grace that establishes and renews the relationship between God and his people. The scope of this commentary is defined by its focus on the religious significance of the Book of Exodus.

By definition a commentary is a secondary source; it *comments* on something else. The primary source, to which this commentary is only a companion, is of course the Bible, and specifically the Book of Exodus. The proper use of a secondary source requires constant attention to the primary one. The Revised Standard Version of the Bible is regularly quoted here, because it is a reliable and readily-available translation. Occasionally reference is made to some feature in the Hebrew original, when the point is not clear in translation.

Those who write commentaries on the Bible, perhaps even more than other authors, draw upon the work of those who wrote before them. To acknowledge this is to recognize that the interpretation of the Scriptures is not the task of isolated individuals, but of a community—not necessarily defined by ecclesiastical or confessional boundaries, but by a common search for the meaning of the text. Especially a commentary like this one, written to provide guidance for those who are not specialists, will seek to incorporate the results of this community endeavor.

Because the character of this commentary makes the use of extensive footnotes inappropriate, it is important to acknowledge at the outset those works to which I am most indebted. First and foremost is *The Book of Exodus: A Critical Theological Commentary* by Brevard Childs. In addition to providing a wealth of information about textual and literary matters, this volume surveys the history of the interpretation of the Book of Exodus, and examines each section in its wider context in the Old Testament and in the whole Bible. The repeated emphasis on the theological significance of the text in its final form has been of particular help. Those familiar with Childs' work will recognize the extent of its influence on the following pages.

Another large volume which has been of considerable use is Ulrich Cassuto's *A Commentary on the Book of Exodus.* Although less comprehensive in its treatment of historical-critical matters (indeed, Cassuto was not in sympathy with the main trends in that area of biblical scholarship), it shares Childs' regard for the integrity of the final form of the biblical text, and is especially sensitive in its treatment of literary style and expression.

Two smaller books have also proven valuable in preparing this commentary. One of them, Moshe Greenberg's *Understanding Exodus*, deals only with the first eleven chapters. The other is *Das Buch Exodus* by Erich Zenger, unfortunately available only in German.

These are the books most frequently consulted in writing this commentary, and to which my indebtedness will perhaps be most readily apparent. But others are no less important in having long since shaped my understanding of its subject. In this regard, I would mention especially the exegesis of the

Book of Exodus by my teacher J. Coert Rylaarsdam in Volume II of *The Interpreter's Bible*, and the classic historical-critical study by Martin Noth, *Exodus: A Commentary*. All of these works, and a small selection of others, are listed in the bibliography which is provided for those who wish to continue their study.

Thanks are due Concordia College in Moorhead, Minnesota, for the sabbatical during which most of the work on this book was done, and to Trinity Lutheran Seminary in Columbus, Ohio, for a term as Visiting Professor, which included the opportunity to teach a course in Exodus. I am grateful to the University of Durham, England, for the generous hospitality extended to me during my months as a Honorary Research Fellow there. Friends in these places and elsewhere, along with members of my family, have given help and encouragement for which no words of thanks could suffice.

Introduction

1. Is Exodus a book?

This is a commentary on the Book of Exodus. The choice of subject rests on the assumption that Exodus is "a book in the usual sense—a self-contained piece of literature with a beginning and an end representing a deliberately defined segment of experience" (Greenberg, *Understanding Exodus*, p.2). Such an assumption should not go unexamined.

It must be acknowledged that Exodus is not completely self-contained, but is part of a larger work known as the Pentateuch or Torah ("Law"). This larger work consists of Genesis, Exodus, Leviticus, Numbers, and Deuteronomy. There is a sense in which the whole Pentateuch constitutes a single "book," of which Exodus is only one of the components. Indeed, the Pentateuch itself is part of a much larger work, the Bible, which can also legitimately be called a "book."

Not only is Exodus part of a larger unit, it is itself composed of several smaller blocks of material. There is, as we shall see, something called "the Book of the Covenant" (20:22—23:33), as well as other clearly-defined segments such as the Ten Commandments (20:1-17) or the Song at the Sea (15:1-18). These can be treated independently as little "books" in their own right.

Nevertheless, the view taken here is that Exodus *is* "a book in the usual sense." It represents "a deliberately defined segment of experience," namely Yahweh's liberation of Israel and his establishment of a special relationship with those he has freed. It has a "beginning"—a prologue that does not simply start where Genesis leaves off, but recapitulates and then makes a fresh start. It also has an "end"—an epilogue which does not lead directly into Leviticus, but rounds off the immediately preceding account by summarizing its eventual outcome. Exodus begins with Israel in bondage in Egypt, helpless, oppressed, and hopeless. It ends with Israel free and on its way to a land of its own, accompanied by its God. Between the prologue and the epilogue is a story about divine initiative, human weakness and sin, and divine forgiveness and renewal. All the parts are drawn together to take their appropriate places in this "self-contained piece of literature."

Thus the Book of Exodus is an appropriate subject for a commentary. We shall try not to lose sight of the larger works of which Exodus is part, nor of the smaller units of which it is composed. But our chief goal is to understand *this* book and its message.

2. What kind of book?

If the Book of Exodus were to be given a place of its own on the shelf of a library or bookstore, in which section would it belong? Some categories can be easily excluded: it is obviously not a cookbook (despite the quails and manna!) or a physics text. It is not so easy, however, to settle on just one label. Yet it is important to do so, for we bring different attitudes, assumptions, and expectations to different kinds of writing. A lyric poem calls for a different frame of mind than a legal contract, and a spy novel for a different one than an article in a medical journal. Lack of clarity about what we are reading results in failure to understand.

Part of the reason for our difficulty with Exodus, in this regard, is that it contains many different kinds of writing. For example, there are genealogies (6:14-25), but it would not be accurate to call Exodus a book of genealogies. There is poetry (ch. 15), but the entire book is clearly not a poem. There are many laws, but the first 19 chapters certainly do not consist of legal material.

Viewed in its entirety, the Book of Exodus is a story with a plot. That being so, the best general designation for it is *narrative*. The varied contents are linked together by the narrative as it moves from beginning to end. Narrative is, however, a very broad designation. Can we be more specific?

The alternatives most likely to occur to us, so far as narrative is concerned, are *fiction* and *history*; is Exodus fiction, or is it history? But these alternatives are not adequate for this book. Exodus is not fiction, because it is a record of the historical experience of a people. But it is also not history in the modern sense of historical reporting.

The events that underlie the book were experienced as God's gracious acts of salvation. Beginning with the eyewitnesses, and continuing across the centuries, successive generations of Israelites reflected on the meaning of these events and drew out their implications from many different perspectives. They told and retold the story, convinced that through this act of remembrance each generation experienced anew God's deliverance and the establishment of his covenant. The setting in which the story was told was the community gathered for worship and the purpose was the strengthening of the community's faith. The Book of Exodus is the culmination of this proclaiming activity. As narrative, therefore, it resembles the first four books of the New Testament, except that the period of time between underlying events and final writing is much briefer in the case of Matthew, Mark, Luke, and John. In identifying the kind of literature represented by the Book of Exodus, it is helpful to borrow a term usually associated with New Testament studies, and think of it as a "gospel."

3. The formation of the book.

The proclaiming activity of which the Book of Exodus is the culmination has a long and varied history. It tells a story which has its setting in a certain time and place, and which was told and retold in succeeding generations. As the circumstances of the people changed, so did the way in which the story was told. Fresh perspectives, emphases, and applications emerged and others receded into the background. The old story, we might say, went through numerous "new editions." The Book of Exodus contains material drawn from several earlier stages, and constitutes a "final edition."

An awareness that such a process lies behind the book is important for our purposes, and reference is made to it in the comments on a number of passages. By way of illustration, we will take a closer look at the subject in relation to one especially suitable section of the Book of Exodus (13:17—14:31). But we will not otherwise undertake any detailed and systematic treatment of the subject. To do so would involve literary and historical considerations that are outside the scope of this commentary. Those who wish to pursue the matter will find ample information in the volumes listed in the bibliography.

It may be useful, however, in view of the importance attached to it in many studies, to summarize the formation of the Book of Exodus as it has been reconstructed by biblical scholars over the past two centuries and more. Some words of caution are in order. First, to present the evidence that provides the basis for the reconstruction would take us far beyond the limits appropriate to a summary of this kind; readers who wish to examine the evidence should consult the works suggested in the bibliography. Second, since the evidence is virtually all internal, any reconstruction is necessarily a hypothesis and must be kept open to revision or replacement. Third, while there is general agreement that the book was formed in the manner broadly described in the first paragraph of this section, many of the particulars are the subject of continuing discussion and debate. The following summary describes an understanding of the process which has long held a large measure of scholarly assent, and may serve as an orientation for the reader who is unfamiliar with the subject.

The formation of the Book of Exodus must be treated together with that of the larger work of which it is part. Some scholars have considered this larger work to include the first four books of the Bible (the "Tetrateuch"), and others the first six (the "Hexateuch"). The traditional view is that the first *five* books (the "Pentateuch") constitute a single group. The question is not a crucial one for our summary.

Neither the Book of Exodus, nor the other books with which it is associated, gives any direct information about the author, the date or place of his activity, the audience for which he wrote, or the way in which he went about his task. There is evidence to suggest, however, that he was among those Jews who struggled for generations, after the return to Judea from the Babylonian Exile in 538 B.C., to reestablish and strengthen their community life within the Persian Empire. This means that the author wrote some seven or eight hundred years after the events about which the Book of Exodus tells. But he was linked to those events by a tradition which had preserved their memory and interpreted their meaning throughout the intervening centuries. It was a dynamic tradition, faithful to what was handed on from the past, but constantly relating it to the changing conditions of the present. It provided him with the sources from which he fashioned a work designed to meet the needs of the community in his day.

The following major sources are usually identified as making an appearance in the Book of Exodus (though they can first be traced in Genesis and continue on into the following books as well). They constitute the earlier "editions" of the story. All of them utilized still earlier material, largely or entirely oral. But each of them had its own point of view, its own adaptation of the message, appropriate to the situation of the community at the time when it was proclaimed.

J, the Yahwistic (or Jahvistic) source. This is largely narrative material, thought to have been compiled in Jerusalem during the United Monarchy, about 950 B.C.

E, the Elohistic source. This is also largely narrative, thought to have been compiled in the Northern Kingdom after the division of the monarchy, about 850 B.C. The material identified as E is more fragmentary than J, a feature usually explained as resulting from a combined edition (JE) having been made in the Southern Kingdom after the fall of the North in 721 B.C., with J as its basis and E used merely to supplement it. Some scholars, however, doubt whether E ever existed as an independent body of material.

P, the Priestly source. While this also contains narrative material, it has quantities of ritual legislation and genealogical lists, of which the priests would be the natural custodians. It is thought to have been compiled during and soon after the Babylonian Exile about 550-500 B.C. Many scholars consider that the final form of the Pentateuch (including the Book of Exodus) issued from this priestly circle.

These major sources do not exhaust what was available to the author of the Book of Exodus. The Ten Commandments and the Book of the Covenant are two examples of material which was apparently not part of J, E, or P, but which the author knew and incorporated into his work.

That so much of the Book of Exodus is drawn from earlier sources raises the question of whether it is justifiable to use the term "author" at all. Some scholars have in fact preferred to refer to a Redactor (R) or editor, whose contribution was a more or less mechanical gathering of traditional material. Others, however, consider that the book as we now have it exhibits an overarching unity and a coherent point of view which have governed the selection, arrangement, and linking together of the contents. For the production of such a work, authorship is a suitable designation.

The formation of the Book of Exodus remains under investigation, and it is unlikely that any one hypothesis will account for all the evidence and satisfy all the scholars. But there is no question that a complex development lies behind the present book, and to know that is important for everyone who studies it. Such an awareness helps us to understand why there is a considerable diversity within the larger unity of the book, and saves us from attempting to harmonize everything in a vain effort to make the contents more uniform than the author intended. More important, it helps us to see that the proclamation is dynamic, not static. It always strikes a delicate balance between the traditions of the past and the changing needs of the present. It calls God's people both to faithfulness and to freedom.

4. Key Theological Themes.

Because this commentary is directed primarily to the religious significance of the Book of Exodus, it is appropriate that we note at the outset some of the most important motifs that appear in it regarding God and his relationship to his people. These may be grouped under two assertions, corresponding to the two main parts of the book. The first is that God is the Deliverer; the second, that he is the Covenant-Maker.

God is the Deliverer. This assertion includes the theme, frequently encountered throughout the Bible, that God acts especially on behalf of the weak and powerless. Our story opens on Israel in Egypt, a group of resident aliens who once enjoyed favorable status but have now fallen under oppression by their powerful host nation. Israel's helplessness in the face of Egyptian exploitation is depicted in vivid terms. It is in response to their expression of utter despair that God turns his face toward them: "And the people of Israel groaned under their bondage, and cried out for help, and their cry under bondage came up to God" (2:23).

A related theme is that God delivers those who are unworthy and utterly without merit. Nothing is said to suggest that the people of Israel in Egypt know God, or worship him, or conduct themselves in such a way as to deserve his favor. From the time that Moses first approaches them in the name of this God who has heard their cry, they doubt and drag their feet and complain. Even after they have been brought out of the land of Egypt, they continue their rebellious ways. "I have seen this people," God says to Moses on one particularly memorable occasion, "and behold, it is a stiff-necked people" (32:9).

Also related to the assertion that God is the Deliverer is the theme that God works through quite ordinary and sometimes disobedient human beings. When we first meet Moses, he is presented as an impetuous and vulnerable person. He remains, even when summoned by God to lead his people, a singularly unwilling and timid leader. It is true that, because of what God accomplishes through him, he assumes genuinely heroic stature. But at the end of his life he must hear God say to him, "Because you did not revere me as holy in the midst of the people of Israel . . . you shall see the land before you, but you shall not go there, into the land which I give to the people of Israel" (Deut. 32:51-52).

Another related theme is that God is Lord over nations and over nature. Pharaoh commands the forces of the greatest world power of his day, but all of his awesome strength is of no avail against God, when God acts to deliver his people. The weapons God turns against Pharaoh and his forces are drawn from the world of nature: reptiles, insects, and diseases figure in the plagues, and the waters of the sea bring about the decisive defeat. Furthermore, the scanty resources of the wilderness are marvelously augmented as God provides for his people during their years of wandering.

Finally, God's deliverance is the central theme of Israel's worship. The great religious festivals prescribed in the Book of Exodus—Passover, Unleavened Bread, Consecration of the Firstborn—have other emphases as well. Not least among them is thanksgiving for fertility: of the soil, the flocks, and the people themselves. But far ahead of all other considerations is the celebration of those great events by which God set his people free: "And when in time to come your son asks you, 'What does this mean?' you shall say to him, 'By strength of hand the LORD brought us out of Egypt, from the house of bondage' " (13:14).

God is the Covenant-Maker. A major theme included in this assertion is that God takes the initiative in establishing the relationship with those who are to be his people. The term "covenant" can be used of agreements mutually entered into by equal partners, but that is emphatically not the kind of bond portrayed in the Book of Exodus. Not only does God deliver Israel without laying any preliminary requirements on them; he takes all the necessary steps to create the ties that will bind Israel to him permanently. In the opening scene at Mount Sinai, where the covenant is ratified, it is made clear beyond any doubt that God is in charge and will remain so.

Complementary to this is the theme that God calls for a response on the part of those whom he has delivered. The people of Israel are not to remain passive recipients of the divine grace. There were no prerequisites for deliverance (or it would not have been an act of grace), but now God's law is made known to those who have been set free. "How will you respond to what I have done for you?" is the unspoken question. The covenant is complete when the people have answered (three times!), "All that the LORD has spoken we will do" (19:8; 24:3, 7).

Tragically, God's people do not keep their promise. That becomes the occasion for introducing another theme related to the assertion that God is the Covenant-Maker: unfaithfulness to God is violation of the relationship and brings divine judgment. The great compassion with which God hears the cry of Israel in bondage has a stark contrast in the dreadful wrath with which he sees them turn away from him while they are still at Sinai, and worship a golden image. The utter serious

ness with which God confronts the disobedience and rebellion of his people cannot be omitted from the portrayal of the
covenant.

Unfaithfulness brings judgment, but repentance is followed
by forgiveness. That is still another theme presented in the
Book of Exodus. Indeed, God's mercy to sinners is so great
that he often seems to overlook their sin; witness his patience
in the face of Israel's frequent murmuring in the wilderness.
Even when their idolatry shatters the covenant beyond any
human possibility of repair, God heeds the intercessions of
Moses and the appeals of his people, and restores the broken
bond.

A final theme related to the assertion that God is the
Covenant-Maker is that he is with his people wherever they
go. In a certain sense, Israel is said to be aware of his presence
from the time he first sets in motion those events which lead
to their escape from Egypt. But it is only when the people
come to Mount Sinai that they experience this presence fully:
after elaborate preparation, "Moses brought the people out of
the camp to meet God; and they took their stand at the foot of
the mountain" (19:17). Israel cannot stay at Mount Sinai
always, however. So God provides the instructions for a portable sanctuary, the tabernacle, "that I may dwell in their
midst" (25:8). When at last the tabernacle is completed, God
fills it with his glory, and the Book of Exodus ends with God
and his people on their way together.

These, then, are some key theological motifs of the book.
We turn now to the story.

Part I

God Delivers Israel
from Bondage

A People in Bondage

1. Israel's initial circumstances in Egypt (1:1-7).

The Book of Exodus begins with a prologue that points both backward and forward. These opening verses point *backward* by first giving the names of the sons of Israel who came to Egypt. In so doing, they direct our attention back to those chapters in the first book of the Bible that tell of the "descent into Egypt." It was Jacob (also called "Israel") who, as head of the family, brought his household and his sons' households from Canaan to Egypt. He had originally only sent for food to be brought from Egypt, because there was a famine in Canaan. But he discovered that his long-lost son Joseph, through a remarkable series of adventures, had become a high official in the Egyptian government. So Jacob was persuaded to bring the entire family to settle in Egypt.

This look backward is a reminder that Jacob and his family came to Egypt under highly favorable circumstances. Thanks to Joseph's exalted position, the rest of the family entered with the approval and under the patronage of the Pharaoh, the king of Egypt.

The prologue points *forward* by referring to the death of Joseph (whose high office has given security to his family) and of the entire generation that came down into Egypt. The book of Genesis ends with the report of Joseph's death, and the repetition here in these verses makes it clear that one era is coming to an end and another is about to begin. Thus our attention is directed to the story that will be unfolded in the following chapters. Before turning to that story, however, the prologue tells us what the good years in Egypt have brought to Jacob's offspring. What they have brought is, in a word, *growth*. The twelve sons of Israel have become the numerous descendants of Israel.[1]

Their growth in numbers is a blessing from God. That is what follows from the stories in Genesis about the patriarchs, the ancestors of those who went down into Egypt. A major theme of those stories is the promise of blessing, including the blessing of many descendants. It is an element in the words God first spoke to Abraham (then still called Abram) when he summoned him from his country and his kindred and his father's house (Gen. 12:1-3, 7). It is repeated to Abraham more forcefully on later occasions; for example, God "brought him outside and said, 'Look toward heaven, and number the stars, if you are able to number them . . . So shall your descendants be' " (Gen. 15:5). The same blessing is promised to Isaac (Gen. 26:2-5) and to Jacob (Gen. 35:11-12). In Egypt God has fulfilled his promise.

Yet the promised blessing is not completely fulfilled. It included not only the blessing of many descendants, but also the blessing of a land of their own and nationhood. This element is prominent in the initial call of Abraham: "I will make of you a great nation . . . To your descendants I will give this land." It regularly accompanies each renewal of the promise of descendants. But in Egypt this promise has not been fulfilled.

Thus Israel's circumstances in Egypt reflect a promise in part fulfilled and in part still pending. Later generations of

---

[1]Several terms are used in the Book of Exodus for this group which sojourns in Egypt. The variety is reflected, though not with consistency, in the words of our English translation: "sons of Israel, descendants of Israel, people of Israel, Hebrews." The terms are not used arbitrarily; for example, they are often called "Hebrews" when being spoken of by others or in relation to others. In our study, we shall not aim at complete consistency, but shall try to use the expressions most appropriate to the particular passages being discussed.

Israelites, hearing or reading the story, would know that the
twelve sons of Jacob represent the twelve tribes of Israel, and
would be led to reflect on their own situation. For the people
of God continually experience both the presence and the absence of his promised blessing, and live in both gratitude and
anticipation.

Indeed, in this respect the whole human race can see itself
reflected in Israel. That is the hint given in the statement, "All
the offspring of Jacob were seventy persons" (Exod. 1:5).
There seems to be a deliberate echo here of the tradition that
there were seventy members of the family of Noah from
whom, after the flood, the whole human race descended
(Gen. 10).

That the story introduced by the prologue concerns the
whole human race is also suggested in another way. Israel's
growth in Egypt is described in such a manner as to reflect the
purpose that God announced for men and women at the time
of their creation. Here we are told that "the descendants of Israel were fruitful and increased greatly; they multiplied and
grew exceedingly strong; so that the land was filled with
them" (v. 7). This list of five verbs resembles a similar list of
five verbs in Genesis 1:28 which tells of the creation of human
beings: "And God blessed them, and God said to them, 'Be
fruitful and multiply, and fill the earth and subdue it; and have
dominion....'"

It will be instructive to compare these lists closely, and this
can best be done if they are set side by side:

Genesis 1:28	Exodus 1:7
be fruitful	were fruitful
multiply	increased greatly
fill [the earth]	multiplied
subdue	grew ... strong
have dominion	[land] was filled

Comparison shows that the lists, although similar, are not
identical. The first three verbs of Genesis 1:28, all of which
have to do with growth in numbers, appear in Exodus

1:7—but in the first, third, and fifth positions. Inserted between them are two additional verbs that reinforce the idea of
growth.

What this implies is that one part of God's purpose for
humanity—that they should be many—has been abundantly
fulfilled in Israel during the years in Egypt. But is that the entirety of the divine intention? The last two verbs in Genesis
1:28 have to do not with growth but with sovereignty:
"subdue," "have dominion." God also wants men and women
to be free and responsible inhabitants of the world in which he
has placed them. These verbs are not included in Exodus 1:7.
This part of God's purpose for humanity has not been fulfilled
in Israel during the years in Egypt. Numerous as the offspring
of Jacob have become, they are still resident aliens in a foreign
land.[2]

Thus the prologue to the Book of Exodus tells us what has
been accomplished in the era that is coming to an end, and
awakens our expectation for what is still to be accomplished.
We are led to expect that the story that follows will tell of
how this representative people, made numerous by God's
grace, will be made free and responsible as well.

2. The change in Israel's circumstances (1:8-22).

Before things get better, however, they often get worse. So
it was with this family. As resident aliens in Egypt they had
something less than full sovereignty, to be sure; they were not
a fully free and responsible people. But at least they were safe;
at least their condition was conducive to an increase in their
population. Now all that was about to change—for the worse.

The favorable circumstances of Jacob's descendants had
rested entirely on Joseph's high office. Those circumstances
could continue even after Joseph's death, as long as there were

[2]This point is developed in an article by James S. Ackerman, "The Literary Context of the Moses Birth Story," in *Literary Interpretations of Biblical Narratives*, edited
by Kenneth R. R. Gros Louis (Nashville: Abingdon Press, 1974).

Pharoahs who remembered with gratitude his services to Egypt. The appearance of a Pharoah who "did not know Joseph" (v. 8) signalled less favorable circumstances to come.

Considerable scholarly effort has been devoted to the attempt to identify this king "who did not know Joseph," and thus establish an approximate date for the events narrated here. The major clue is provided by the reference to Pithom and Rameses as the store-cities built by the oppressed Israelites (v. 11). There is evidence (not altogether conclusive) that these cities were built under Seti I (1308-1290 B.C.) and Rameses II (1290-1224 B.C.). If so, then Seti I may well have been the Pharaoh of the oppression, and Rameses II the Pharaoh of the Exodus.

Such historical considerations are important, because they remind us that the proclamation of the Book of Exodus is firmly rooted in the real world of time and space. Two points should be kept in mind, however. First, specific identification seems not to be important to the biblical author; at any rate, he does not provide the name of any Egyptian king. Second, an undue emphasis on the identity of particular monarchs undercuts the symbolic character of the Pharaoh in the narrative.

This leads us to the matter of the role played by the new king of Egypt in the story that follows. He is not simply one human being among others who encounters the God of Israel and is treated perhaps a little unfairly. As Pharaoh, he was viewed in Egyptian thought as the son of the god Re, and therefore himself an incarnation of deity. The Book of Exodus does not portray him as actually divine, of course. But it does portray him as the ruler of a great world power, who sets himself against the God of Israel and uses all the might at his command in an effort to prevent the fulfillment of God's purpose for his people. In our story he is God's chief opponent—we might call him the anti-God—and it will be helpful to keep this representative role in mind as we consider how he is dealt with in the episodes that follow.

The new king notes how numerous this group of resident

aliens has become. He does not view this growth as it was presented in the prologue, however. It is not to him a mark of divine favor and a partial fulfillment of God's purpose. It is, rather, a threat to himself and to the Egyptians. "Behold, the people of Israel are too many and too mighty for us," he says to his people (v. 9). It is significant that the first time the descendants of Jacob are called a "people" is in the words of this hostile ruler. In his mind they have become a people who pose a threat to the people of Egypt.

The threat, however, is purely hypothetical. It is true that the people of Israel are resident aliens. It is true that they live in a frontier district (the "land of Goshen"). And it is true that they have become numerous. But they have done nothing to harm the Egyptians. The action Pharaoh is about to propose is intended to forestall what his paranoid mind imagines might take place. He fears that the people of Israel might multiply even more; he fears that, in case of war, they might join the enemy; and he fears that they might run away. To his way of thinking, action ought to be taken against those who are innocent, just because there is a possibility that they may become guilty.

He proposes, therefore, that the Egyptians "deal shrewdly" (v. 10) with this group in their midst. There is an echo here of the reputation for wisdom that Egypt possessed in the world of that day. Egypt's ancient origins, stretching far back into antiquity; its overwhelming monuments, among them the pyramids; its mysterious hieroglyphic writing; its large and powerful priestly class—all of these evoked an understandable awe among neighboring nations. Indeed, the action that follows Pharaoh's proposal is shrewd, for it is designed to get the greatest possible benefit out of the presence of this ethnic minority, while at the same time exhausting them in order to reduce their numbers. There is, however, irony in the biblical report of Pharaoh's words. Shrewdly as the Egyptians deal with the Israelites, their dealings do not accomplish what they intend.

The measures against the Israelites are undertaken in four stages. First, the Egyptians collaborate with Pharaoh in putting the Israelites to forced labor. Nothing is said to suggest that the Israelites resist in any way; they build two "store-cities" for Pharaoh. At the same time, far from dwindling away, their numbers increase, and it is implied that this continues to be the case through each succeeding stage of Egyptian action. Furthermore, the act of oppression, undertaken in response to Pharaoh's fears, does not banish fears but only broadens them: "And the Egyptians were in dread of the people of Israel" (v. 12). It can be seen, in view of what was noted earlier, that no earthly power can cancel the purpose of God, once he has undertaken to fulfill it. He has given the people of Israel increase, and they continue to grow. He has not given them sovereignty, however, and the longer they are in Egypt the further they are from free and responsible existence.

The second stage in the measures taken against the Israelites is also carried out by the Egyptian people. Perhaps it is simply an intensification of the first stage, but it marks a definite change in status for the Israelites: formerly they were resident aliens, but now they have clearly become slaves, in fact if not in name: "So they made the people of Israel serve with rigor, and made their lives bitter with hard service, in mortar and brick, and in all kinds of work in the field; in all their work they made them serve with rigor" (vv. 13-14). Although it is difficult to express in translation, there is a fivefold repetition in this sentence of words formed from the same Hebrew root; they are, in our English translation, "serve, service, work, work, serve."[3] This repetition reminds us of the five verbs at the end of the prologue, and deliberately contrasts the absence of sovereignty (the unfulfilled part of God's promise) with the presence of a large population (the fulfilled part).

The first two of the steps taken against the Israelites are

---

[3]It frequently happens, in Hebrew, that a number of words, both nouns and verbs, are formed from the same root word. Their close relationship can easily be seen in the original, but it is difficult and often impossible to show this in an English translation.

carried out by the Egyptians, with no reference to any specific instructions from Pharaoh (beyond his initial proposal to "deal shrewdly with them"). After those measures have proven ineffective, Pharaoh takes charge more directly. In this third stage, he commands the midwives who assist the Hebrew women in childbirth to kill all male children born to them. This is, of course, an undercover operation, and the apparent secrecy of the arrangements suggests an unwillingness on Pharaoh's part to admit to the failure of his shrewdness thus far.

These midwives play an important role in the story. They are called "the Hebrew midwives," but it is not clear whether they are themselves Israelites, or whether they are Egyptians who serve the Israelites in this way. It may be that the possibility of their being Egyptian is supported by such features as the conversations between them and Pharaoh, the special note made of the fact that they feared God and disobeyed Pharaoh, and the further special note that God then blessed the midwives in the same way that he continued to bless the people of Israel. If we are to think of them as Egyptian, then we are presented here with a hint that Pharaoh's intentions are being undermined by those within his own nation.

More important than the question of the midwives' nationality is the fact that they are women. The significance of this goes beyond the rather obvious fact that we would expect midwives in ancient societies to be female. For women were then among the powerless of the world, at least so far as directing the destiny of nations was concerned. Yet here is the first of a series of women who, for all their powerlessness, frustrate Pharaoh's schemes against the people of Israel. Rather than submit to an immoral order, even though that order comes from the very top, they engage in an act of civil disobedience which gives them strength and influence far beyond that which belongs to their "place."

Also significant is the way in which the midwives succeed in disobeying Pharaoh without incurring punishment for having done so. They outsmart him. They tell him a cock-and-bull story about the Hebrew women being so much more vigorous than the Egyptian women (note the put-down) as not to require the services of midwives. And he believes them! Thus the ruler of the wisest nation on earth, who has proposed to deal shrewdly, is outwitted by representatives of those who seemed weakest in worldly might.

Pharaoh's final stage is a public command to his people to kill every son born to the Hebrews. Where shrewdness and secrecy fail, nothing is left to a despot but an open appeal to violence. On that note, the first chapter of Exodus ends.

At the end of this opening chapter, we look back at what we have seen. We have had our attention directed backward to the narratives in Genesis, which tell of a God who intends for his people to be both numerous and free. We have had it made clear to us that the first part of that intention is being abundantly fulfilled, even in the face of great obstacles. But we have also been given to understand that the second part of God's intention has not only gone unfulfilled, but seems much further from fulfillment as the people of Israel sink more and more deeply into slavery in Egypt.

Nevertheless, a pattern is emerging that leads us to expect further developments. There is a series of references to the growth of the people of Israel (vv. 7, 12, 20). There is also a series of references to measures taken against the people of Israel (vv. 11, 13, 16, 22). None of these measures is successful in reducing Israel's numbers, but they increase in severity in such a way that clearly things must eventually come to a head. From forced labor to virtual slavery to private disposal of the newly-born to public slaughter of infants—matters can hardly continue to escalate in this way! We expect a break in the story. It comes in Exodus 2.

Before turning to the next chapter, however, there is a question to be considered. What is the reason for this delay between the fulfillment of God's intention that his people be many and his intention that they be free? It is easy to see why

Jacob and his sons and their households were led into Egypt
from Canaan: they escaped the famine, and their lives were
preserved. And it is not hard to understand why they re-
mained there while circumstances were favorable: they grew
to be a numerous people. But what, in the providence of God,
was the purpose of the suffering inflicted on them by the "new
king . . . who did not know Joseph"?

The first chapter of Exodus does not address this question.
But references elsewhere in Exodus (and also in Deuteronomy) point the way to an answer. From its time in bondage, Israel learned a lesson about the treatment of others, especially
those who are outsiders or otherwise weak and helpless. "You
shall not wrong a stranger or oppress him, for you were strangers in the land of Egypt. You shall not afflict any widow or
orphan" (22:21-22). "You shall not oppress a stranger; you
know the heart of a stranger, for you were strangers in the
land of Egypt" (23:9; see also Deut. 5:12-15; 15:12-15;
16:11-12). Thus, out of the remembrance of suffering came
that sense of identification with those who suffer which
would shape Israel's practice of justice in generations to come.

A Leader Prepared

1. The birth of Moses (2:1-10).

We have observed that the first chapter of the Book of Exodus begins with the offspring of Jacob living in favorable circumstances in Egypt, continues with the change in those circumstances to a condition of bondage, and ends with an intense escalation of the suffering to which they are subjected. We expect the second chapter in some way to relieve the tension that has been built up. Our first impression, however, is that it simply changes the subject. A man and a woman, both descendants of Levi, marry and have a son. Only gradually do we discover just how much this has to do with what has gone before.

The man and woman are quite ordinary individuals among the Hebrew people; at any rate, their names are not given when we are first introduced to them (although later on, in 6:18-20, names are provided) and the father has no further part in the story. It seems at first that the son whose birth is described is this couple's firstborn, although we soon find that there is an older sister (v. 4); and eventually an older brother, Aaron, makes his appearance (4:14). The child, in any case, is born in difficult times—a fact that links this chapter to the preceding one. Pharaoh's command to his people—"Every son that is born to the Hebrews you shall cast into the Nile" (1:22)—makes the child's survival uncertain, to say the least.

At this point the child's mother, although still without a name, emerges as a remarkable woman, a worthy successor to the midwives who foiled one of Pharaoh's earlier schemes. First she hides the child for three months. Then, when that is no longer practical, she carries out an ingenious scheme. There is a trace of humor in her actions, for she puts the child where Pharaoh had commanded male infants to be cast—into the Nile. But of course she does not throw the child in to drown; she places him in a basket designed to protect him from drowning.

The basket deserves a closer look. It is described in such a way as to signal the special importance of the child for whom it was prepared. The word here translated "basket" (v. 3) is used elsewhere in the Bible only of Noah's ark, another rescue vessel made waterproof by the use of pitch. We are reminded in this way of one who, earlier in the biblical story, is saved from death by drowning so as to be the means of survival for the human race. The child being placed in this little ark (so it is hinted) is destined to do something similar for his people, who are threatened with annihilation in the waters of the Nile.

The child, whose own chances for survival seem so small, is rescued by the daughter of Pharaoh. She sees the basket, takes pity on the crying infant, and recognizes him as "one of the Hebrews' children" (v. 6). Her action allies her, although she is unaware of it, with the midwives and the child's mother. The midwives disobeyed Pharaoh because they feared God. The mother eluded his decree because she loved the child she had borne. The pity felt by the Egyptian princess is not so powerful a motive as those, but her high station makes it possible for her, simply out of pity, to save this one Hebrew child. As things work out, she too will have played a major part in frustrating Pharaoh's intentions. The irony is that Pharaoh's own edict provided the occasion for Moses' rescue and adoption by Pharaoh's daughter.

Still another woman—or, perhaps more accurately, a girl—now enters the picture. She is the baby's sister. Her name also is not given, though later in the story we are told of a sister whose name is Miriam (15:20). She has been watching from a distance to see what would happen to the child, and approaches Pharaoh's daughter to offer assistance. In the conversation that follows, the Egyptian princess is presented in a rather ambiguous light. On the one hand, we view her favorably because of her pity for what she knows is a Hebrew child. On the other hand, she is a representative of the oppressing power, and we are pleased and amused when she is hoodwinked by the child's family. For the sister offers to find a nurse for this baby the princess has decided to keep, and is given permission with a curt command: "Go!" (v. 8). The "nurse" brought to her is, of course, the baby's mother (though the princess does not know it). It is a good joke, then, when Pharaoh's daughter hires the mother to care for the baby, paying her wages to do the very thing she most wants to do.

Eventually the time comes when the child no longer requires a nurse. The youngster is then brought to Pharaoh's daughter, who adopts him and names him "Moses." The name is probably from an Egyptian word meaning "to bear, give birth." But the biblical account notes the resemblance of the name to the Hebrew word meaning "to draw out, save." This, too, has a superficial appropriateness; as the princess says, "Because I drew him out of the water" (v. 10). In view of how the story will turn out, however, the name serves as a hint that Moses will one day himself draw out others. But it is only a hint. Pharaoh's power, though thwarted in little ways, remains fundamentally unchallenged. God's purpose continues to be frustrated. Israel is still living under oppression. No one could realistically expect that this child could or would bring about a change. If God is going to challenge the entrenched forces of evil, surely he will have to do so in some spectacular way!

2. Moses' intervention and flight to Midian (2:11-22).

We are told nothing of Moses' youth in the Egyptian court. The story turns immediately to the episode in which he seeks to identify with the Hebrews, and in the process cuts himself off from his royal ties. Moses has grown to manhood, and is observing the Hebrews working at the tasks imposed on them. That he is described as going out to "his people" (v. 11) indicates that he already considers himself to be one of them. But now it is said that he "looked on their burdens," and this surely implies more than an objective and dispassionate glance. When he sees an Egyptian beating a Hebrew to death, he is moved to take drastic action. He strikes the Egyptian in the same way (the same Hebrew word is used) and kills him.

Before killing the Egyptian, Moses "looked this way and that" (v. 12). Why does he do this? The most apparent reason is to make sure that he is not observed. This is supported by the fact that he then hides the body, and is afterward surprised and disturbed that the deed is known. But it may also be that he first looks to see whether anyone else will intervene, before taking action himself. He is, after all, a mere bystander with no direct responsibility, whatever his sympathies may be. Where are the Egyptian authorities? Even slaves, however oppressed and overburdened with work, are not usually subjected to arbitrary slaughter—and there is no evidence that the Hebrew being beaten had provoked an attack, or that his attacker had a right to kill him. Or where, for that matter, are the other Hebrews, who might be expected to defend one of their number against unprovoked attack? When it is clear that there is no one else to take action, Moses does so himself. In any case, by looking around first, Moses makes clear that what he does is premeditated, and represents his own firm sympathies.

Moses is being drawn into the situation created by the bondage of his people. This is indicated by the fact that he is back the next day and this time intervenes without hesitation. He sees two Hebrews struggling together, and reproaches the one who is in the wrong. When he does so, he makes a discovery. His deed in killing the Egyptian is known. That in itself is unsettling enough. But Moses also discovers that what he has done has not made him popular with the Hebrews. They do not consider Moses' motive to be one of sympathy for his people or concern for justice. Rather, they think that he is assuming authority over them, and are threatened by it. That is what is implied by the response of the Hebrew reproached by Moses: "Who made you a prince and judge over us? Do you mean to kill me as you killed the Egyptian?" (v. 14).

This is an impudent reply for a Hebrew to make to a member of the Egyptian court. It shows an awareness that Moses is not an Egyptian, and that he has committed a deed which he has tried to conceal. It also anticipates a theme that will appear frequently as the story unfolds: the so-called "rebellion" motif, with Israel repeatedly expressing resentment at Moses' leadership (see, for example, 14:11-12). There is also an irony in the first part of the Hebrew's reply. Nothing has yet been said about what Moses is to become or accomplish. But the point at which the story of his birth is introduced, and the remarkable manner of his preservation from death, hint at the destiny that awaits him. There will be an answer to the question, "Who made you a prince and a judge over us?"

The fact is, however, that Moses has not yet been called to such an office. The Hebrews will be given a leader and delivered from bondage only when God intervenes. He, and he alone, decides the time of his intervention. Moses' act of violence is understandable and well-intentioned. But it is not an expression of obedience to God, and accomplishes nothing.

Thus Moses' deed does not win him the gratitude of his people or rouse them to unite and resist their oppressor. Instead it results in an attempt on Pharaoh's part to kill him. We are not told why Pharaoh should concern himself with the killing of one Egyptian by a member of the royal court. But Moses takes the threat so seriously that he flees the country. Perhaps we are intended to see how Moses' fear of Pharaoh at this stage compares unfavorably with the midwives' fear of God.

Moses flees to "the land of Midian." This is probably not to be understood as a specific country, but as the general area east of Egypt in which were to be found the people known as Midianites. He soon meets, settles with, and marries into a Midianite family. The story of how this came about is rather romantic. Moses, now a fugitive from Egyptian justice, sits down by a well. Seven girls come along and draw water for their father's flock, but are driven away by some shepherds. Moses comes to their rescue and helps them to complete their task. They return home earlier than usual (apparently the delay caused by the bullying shepherds has come to be the expected thing), and their father questions them. When he learns what has happened, he reproaches the girls for not having brought their rescuer home with them. He sends them after Moses, offers him hospitality and a home, and ultimately gives him one of the daughters as a wife.

This episode is reminiscent of two others, both described in the Book of Genesis. One, in Genesis 24, tells of how Abraham's servant stops at a well in a distant country, and there finds a wife for his master's son Isaac. The other, in Genesis 29, tells of how Isaac's son Jacob finds a wife for himself in a similar setting. For all the resemblances, however, a quite different point is being made here than in the two Genesis passages. In Genesis, the emphasis is on the finding of a wife for a patriarch, so that together they may become ancestors of the people of the promise. The episode with Moses has a very different emphasis. It is true that he ends up with a wife. But he has not come to the well in order to seek a wife, and he does not take action there in order to secure one.

Moses' intervention is another expression of that concern for justice which led him to kill the Egyptian who was abusing the Hebrew and to reproach the Hebrew who was wronging his fellow-Hebrew. That he now intervenes a third time, even though his earlier involvements have made him a refugee, shows that it is his very nature to take action on behalf of justice.

Especially interesting is the fact that each occasion involves a different combination of participants. It can be summarized in this way:

Exodus 2:	One doing injustice	One suffering injustice
11-12	Egyptian	Hebrew
13-14	Hebrew	Hebrew
17	Midianite	Midianite

In other words, Moses involves himself not only when his own people are being wronged by others, or when they are doing wrong to one another, but whenever wrong is being done, even among non-Hebrews. His concern for justice is universal, no matter what the cost to himself.

Moses the fugitive from Egypt has found a secure place, because of the gratitude of this Midianite family. Their gratitude contrasts strikingly with the ingratitude of Moses' own people on those earlier occasions. He now has a home, a wife, and—in due time—a son. We might expect the story of Moses to end here; we would not be surprised by the words, "And they lived happily ever after." But we are given a signal that the story is not to end in that way, and that Moses' involvement with his people in Egypt is not over. He names his son "Gershom." Whatever the original meaning of this name (it is probably derived from a word meaning "drive away, banish"), Moses chooses it because it reminds him of the Hebrew phrase "a sojourner there." Thus we are told that Moses thinks of himself as a temporary resident, not a permanent one, in Midian. His future will take him elsewhere: not just to Egypt, where he and his people are also sojourners, but toward a place where they will belong.

3. God's awareness of Israel's plight (2:23-25).

While Moses was in Midian, the king of Egypt died. But that brings no improvement in the lot of the people of Israel. Two more references to their "bondage" remind us of the five-fold repetition of related words in 1:13-14; there has been no change. Perhaps it is this which precipitates a crisis for them. It was this Pharaoh's coming to the throne that brought an end to their earlier favored status. It was he who plunged them into the depths of suffering. Now he is dead, but his death brings no relief. The oppressed people are at the end of their endurance.

Their despair does not result in silent reflection over suffering as a theoretical problem. It issues in groans and cries. Nothing is said to suggest that these laments are directed to anyone in particular. The people seem not to know where to turn for help. Thus it is all the more significant that their cry is said to come up "to God" (v. 23). This is the first reference in the Book of Exodus to any concern on God's part for Israel's plight (the only exception is the passing comment about the blessing the midwives receive because they fear him). But now suffering men and women break the silence with their laments, and cry out for help. They are met by the compassion of God. This is not because they first remember him or turn to him or prove worthy of him. It is solely because he is true to himself and to his promises.

The intensity with which God now turns to Israel is underscored by the repeated use of the noun where a simple pronoun would have been adequate: "God heard . . . God remembered . . . God saw . . . God knew" (vv. 24-25). He is about to enter directly into the story and intervene decisively on behalf of those who suffer. To all outward appearances, nothing has changed. But in reality, a fundamental turning point has been reached.

As we look back over this chapter, we see attention centered on one of the Hebrew children. Preserved from death by the actions of several women, both Hebrew and Egyptian, this child grows to manhood in the Egyptian court but identifies with his oppressed people. Forced to flee, and alienated from Egyptian and Hebrew alike, he settles in a foreign place but remains aware of his status as a temporary resident. Nothing is said of what is to become of this man Moses. But we anticipate that we have not heard the last of him. As for God, at the end of the chapter he is waiting in the wings. Beginning with Exodus 3, he will be very much at the center of the stage.

A Leader Appointed

1. The call of Moses (3:1-15).

We were told, at the end of Exodus 2, about God's awareness of Israel's plight. Following as it does on the story of Moses' early life, it signals some connection between this man and God's concern. But Moses is unaware of it, and goes about his usual business as one who dwells among the Midianites. He tends the flock of his father-in-law.

There are, in the story, some things about the father-in-law which are rather puzzling. This is brought to our attention particularly by the fact that he is here called "Jethro" (v. 1) while in 2:18 he is called "Reuel" (his name is given as "Hobab" in Num. 10:29 and Judg. 4:11). He is consistently designated "the priest of Midian"; but that leaves us wondering why he has so little wealth and prestige that (according to Exod. 2) his seven daughters must water their father's flock and be subjected to repeated harassment by the shepherds. We find no explanation of these matters; apparently Israel's memories of this man were hazy in regard to details. Later on in the story, as we shall see, he will have an important role to play in Moses' leadership over the people of Israel.

As Moses tends the flock, he comes to a place called "Horeb." The description of its location is vague, but it is called "the mountain of God" (v. 1). This may mean that we are to think of it as already a sacred place, even before Moses came there. If that is so, Moses shows no awareness of it; he does not behave with any special reverence until he is told that he is standing on "holy ground" (v. 5). More likely, Horeb is called the mountain of God in anticipation of the great importance it is to have for the faith of Israel.

We come now to one of the best-known of biblical narratives: the story of the burning bush. It is the first of numerous episodes in the Book of Exodus (and the whole Bible) in which God is said to act through natural circumstances. A bush is, of course, something natural. There are desert bushes in the part of the world where Moses was keeping the sheep. Probably such bushes catch fire from time to time or (we might speculate) there may be bushes with foliage that reflects the bright sunlight or flowers that make them look aflame. But such "explanations" are far from the point of the story.

The emphasis is, rather, on the divine activity. The burning bush is the means by which God who is aware of Israel's plight reveals himself to the sojourner who is to be the instrument of Israel's deliverance. The revelation is a matter of both sight and sound. "The angel of the Lord" (v. 2) is not a separate being, sent in place of God himself, but a visible manifestation of God, as is clear from the dialogue that follows. The flame of fire in which the angel appears is a frequent symbol of the divine presence (in the New Testament we have, in Acts 2, the example of the tongues of fire on the heads of the disciples at Pentecost). Moses, however, does not anticipate an encounter with the divine. He is simply curious about this unusual sight. It is not until he is actually addressed by God that the meaning of it becomes clear to him.

Drawn to the bush by his curiosity, Moses hears the word of God. The word begins with a personal address: "Moses, Moses!" (v. 4)—the repetition indicating the urgency of what is to be said. Moses replies, and is commanded to remove his shoes, the customary act of reverence for those who enter a sacred place. Then God introduces himself. He is the God of Israel's ancestors, who gave them promises—promises which have been only partly fulfilled. As at the end of Exodus 2, the word "God" is repeated here in 3:6 where grammar alone would not require it: "The God of Abraham, the God of Isaac, and the God of Jacob." Perhaps this is meant to express God's faithfulness from one past generation to another. Moses' response to this self-introduction is to hide his face. Only now does he become fully aware that he is in the presence of God.

The God of past generations then announces his intention to be the God of the present generation as well. His faithfulness requires an involvement in the life and fortunes of those who are descended from the patriarchs. The verbs with which God expresses his intention—"I have seen . . . have heard . . . know" (v. 7)—echo those of 2:24-25. He is announcing to Moses that it is the plight of the people descended from Abraham, Isaac, and Jacob which is rousing him to new activity on their behalf. They are not just a helpless band of aliens oppressed by the Egyptians. They are "my people" (v. 7).

We have noted that, at the end of Exodus 2, the groaning and crying of the people are not directed anywhere in particular; nevertheless, God receives their lament. This same divine initiative is suggested by the sequence of verbs in 3:7: God first sees the affliction of his people; only then does he hear their cry. God is aware of his people's suffering even before they begin to complain about it.

Something momentous is involved in God's appearance in the burning bush. It involves not only Moses, but the whole people whose sufferings are known to God. "I have come down to deliver them," God announces (v. 8). Behind this expression is the imagery of a God who dwells in the heavens, looks down on human beings upon the earth, and occasionally descends to take part in their activities. Nothing crudely literal is intended, however. Through the language of movement from the heavens to the earth is conveyed the idea of God's involvement in the life of the world. This God is not abstract, aloof, indifferent. He is a God who, motivated by his faithfulness and compassion, "comes down."

The purpose of God's intervention on behalf of his people is twofold: it is "to deliver them" and "to bring them up" (v. 8). The former is the negative side of God's action; his people are delivered "out of the hand of the Egyptians." Salvation is first of all *from* something. The latter is the positive side; his people are brought up "to a good and broad land, a land flowing with milk and honey." Salvation is finally *to* something. From the weight given here to each of these, it is clear that the emphasis is on the positive aspect of salvation. That to which Israel will be brought up is described much more fully than that from which it is to be delivered.

It is especially God's compassion which we see in the work of deliverance. He has had pity on those who have suffered such great affliction at the hand of the Egyptians. It is especially his faithfulness which we see in the work of bringing the people up to a land promised to the ancestors. The list, in v. 8, of the people already in the land appears only once before in the biblical narrative. That is at Genesis 15:19-21, at the end of the passage in which God solemnly announces to Abraham the destiny he has in store for Abraham's descendants. God's appearance to Moses in the burning bush sets in motion the fulfillment of that destiny.

So far, nothing has been said about what role, if any, Moses is to have in what God proposes to do. "Why are you telling all this to me?" we can almost imagine Moses asking. But now comes the summons, and the crucial verse of this section of the story: "Come, I will send you" (v. 10). God will be much more in the foreground in the events to come than he was in the events of the first two chapters. But he will continue to operate through human agents, and Moses in particular is here called to be the one through whom God will deliver his people.

But perhaps God's summons is not as unexpected as we might think. Moses' reply, at any rate, is surprisingly prompt—and it is not all that piety might desire. It is downright abrupt: "Who am I," Moses asks God, "that I should go

to Pharaoh, and bring the sons of Israel out of Egypt?"
(v. 11). Rather than welcoming his call, and gladly assuming
the role of leadership, Moses raises his voice in protest—the
first of five such protests, as we shall see. And even if our piety
is offended, we must recognize his protest as the voice of reality. He is a fugitive in Midian, utterly without status before
either the Egyptians whom he is to oppose or the Israelites
whom he is to lead.

God, who is untouched by Moses' lack of piety, answers
him patiently. First he reminds Moses of what has already
been implied in his previous words. Did God not say "I have
come down" (v. 8) and "I will send you" (v. 10)? The proper
question is not "Who am I that I should go . . . and bring," but
"Who are you that send me?" Now God makes it explicit:
"But I will be with you." Furthermore, he offers Moses a sign:
"This shall be the sign for you, that I have sent you: when you
have brought forth the people out of Egypt, you shall serve
God upon this mountain" (v. 12).

There is a problem in understanding what is meant by the
sign. We would expect it to be something immediate, something that would demonstrate to Moses, before he takes up the
task to which he is being called, that God will truly be with
him as promised. Instead, it appears that the sign is to be something which will *follow* the successful completion of Moses'
mission: namely serving God on the mountain where Moses
now stands.

If such later service is the intended sign, then what God is
saying is that Moses will receive no sign in the usual sense of
the word. That is, he will receive no proof in advance, but will
know that God has been with him when his task is done. This
would be a credible (if not very comforting) way of understanding the verse, except for one difficulty: Moses has not
asked for a sign. It is God who here brings up the matter of a
sign, and it seems unlikely that he would do so only in order to
refuse one in such an indirect way.

There is another possibility for understanding what is being said here. Perhaps the word "this" in the phrase "this shall be the sign for you" does not refer to the latter part of the sentence about serving God upon the mountain. Perhaps it refers, rather, to what Moses is now experiencing. If so, the meaning would be as follows: "This" (namely, my revealing myself to you in the burning bush) "shall be the sign for you, that I have sent you. When you have brought forth the people, you shall serve God upon this mountain."

However this may be, Moses is not persuaded, and he immediately makes a second protest. He now knows this God as the God of Abraham, Isaac, and Jacob. But he anticipates that, if he comes to the people with the claim that he has been sent to them by the God of their fathers, they will want more specific identification. "What is his name?" they will ask (v. 13); how is he to reply?

We should not underestimate the implications of this question. Names were immensely significant in the ancient world. A name was intended to match the character of the one who bore it. To have no name was to have no existence; to have a great name was to exist fully. To speak someone's name was to make the bearer of the name effectively present. In the case of a god, the name gave blessing and protection. To invoke the name of a deity meant to control, in some measure, the power of that deity. To Moses' question about his name, God gives two answers: The first is for Moses himself, and assumes that he is seeking an explanation of the significance of the name. The other is for the people of Israel.

The answer given to Moses is the single phrase "I am who I am" (v. 14). Brief as it is, it has presented a virtually insurmountable obstacle to the understanding of later generations. Because this is the only passage in the Old Testament which attempts to explain the name of God, we cannot gain any help from other references. Of the numerous interpretations which have been offered, none can be said to be conclusive. The one clear point is that a connection is being made between the divine name, which is "Yahweh,"[1] and a Hebrew word with such varied meanings as "be, become, cause to be," and so on. How is the phrase best understood? Passing over the intricacies and uncertainties of the scholarly debate, we can affirm in the light of the entire context that Yahweh is the name of the God who has chosen a people to be his own, is faithful to the relationship he has established with them, and will act to fulfill the purpose he has for them—but who still retains his own sovereign freedom.

The answer Moses is told to give to the people of Israel has two parts. The first is related to the explanation Moses has just received: "Say this to the people of Israel, 'I AM has sent me to you' " (v. 14). Now that Moses knows the significance of the divine name, he will be able to reply to the inquiry of the Israelites. The second part directs Moses to announce the name itself, "Yahweh," to the people, and then to make clear that Yahweh is not a new god, but the God of their fathers.

There is something confusing about this request for God's name. Is the name "Yahweh," which Moses is told to give to the people, now being revealed for the first time? If we look ahead to 6:2-3, we find a statement which strongly supports that view: "God said to Moses, 'I am the LORD [Yahweh]. I appeared to Abraham, to Isaac, and to Jacob, as God Almighty, but by my name the LORD [Yahweh] I did not make myself known to them.' " But we also note that the name Yahweh appears many times in the biblical narrative before Exodus 3, and is frequently said to be spoken by the patriarchs. In fact, in the midst of the stories about the very first human beings, we are told that "At that time men began to call on the name of the LORD [Yahweh]" (Gen. 4:26).

---

[1]The spelling "Yahweh" represents the best scholarly estimation of how the divine name was pronounced in biblical times. In Hebrew manuscripts, only the consonants were written (YHWH). Eventually the practice arose of showing reverence by not pronouncing the name itself, but substituting "the LORD" wherever YHWH was written. This is the origin of the practice, in most English translations (including the Revised Standard Version), of printing "the LORD" wherever the name "Yahweh" should appear. It is a rather misleading practice, since "Yahweh" is not a title like "the LORD," but a proper name. The regular use of that proper name by biblical Israel is obscured by these translations.

It appears that, among the people of Israel, there was more than one view as to when God first revealed to them his personal name, Yahweh. Traces of these varied views have found their way into the Old Testament. What remains constant is Israel's conviction that it is the same God, by whatever name he is called, who works among them from beginning to end. In the story of the call of Moses, Moses is told to announce to the people that the God who has sent him is the God of their fathers; his everlasting name is Yahweh, and that is the name by which they are always to remember him. In other words, they are told his name and its significance, not to satisfy their curiosity but so that they may worship him.

2. Instructions to Moses (3:16 — 4:17).

Yahweh (we shall call him by the name he has just given) has been responding to Moses' protests. Now he begins to give Moses directions about the carrying out of his mission. Moses is first to gather the elders of Israel together; apparently, even in their desperate circumstances, there are still older members of the community who provide a measure of leadership. He is to inform them of what he has learned from Yahweh about Yahweh's intentions for them. Moses is assured that the elders "will hearken to your voice" (3:18). Then Moses and the elders are to go to the king of Egypt. They are to tell him that Yahweh their God has met with them, and are to make a request: "We pray you, let us go on a three days' journey into the wilderness, that we may sacrifice to the LORD our God" (3:18).

This is a surprisingly modest request to put before Pharaoh, in view of Yahweh's announced intention to deliver Israel from bondage to Egypt and bring them up to a land of their own. Perhaps we are to view this as simply the opening move in a long process of negotiation. If so, it would be a way of dis-

covering Pharaoh's attitude in a small matter, before going on
to present him with the large one. Or perhaps we are to view it
as a deception: let Pharaoh give them three days' start, and
they might be able to elude his grasp.

However it is to be viewed, Yahweh immediately informs
Moses that the request will not be granted, and he then alludes
to the long sequence of events which must take place before
Pharaoh lets Israel go. Why, then, should Moses and the elders go to the trouble of appearing before Pharaoh? Apparently the outcome is described in order to reassure Moses, in the
face of coming difficulties, that Yahweh will finally give him
success in his mission. But the difficulties along the way cannot be bypassed. The entire drama must be played out, if Yahweh's deliverance is to have its full effect.

One of the things Yahweh tells Moses to expect is that the
people will not leave Egypt empty-handed. The Israelite
women will ask for jewelry and clothing for their children,
and will receive them from the Egyptian women. These items
will be given willingly, because the Egyptians involved will
look with favor on those who receive them. But it is not clear
that they will be intended by those who give them to be a permanent gift to be taken out of the country. Rather, this is said
to be a way to "despoil" or plunder the Egyptians. Certainly it
is only fair that these oppressed people should leave Egypt
with something to show for their years of servitude, even if
the compensation is far from adequate. More to the point,
however, this is an indication that, after a long struggle, Israel
will emerge victorious, taking with them booty like that col-
lected by a conquering army. At the same time, it constitutes a
good joke played by the departing slaves on their erstwhile
masters.

The words which Yahweh has just spoken to Moses assume
that Moses has now become the leader through whom Yahweh will carry out his intentions for his people. Moses'
response, however, is a third protest, and takes things back
again to an earlier stage: "But behold, they will not believe me

or listen to my voice, for they will say, 'The LORD did not appear to you' " (4:1). It is as if Moses has not heard anything that Yahweh has said about the audience with the king of Egypt and all that is to follow it. He is still hung up on the question of how the Israelites would receive his claim to leadership—a question related to his second protest (3:13), and perhaps also to his first (3:11). This is all the more remarkable in view of Yahweh's clear assurance that "they will hearken to your voice" (3:18). It is difficult to avoid the conclusion that Moses here expresses doubts which directly contradict the divine assurance. We are given one more example, among many in the Bible, of God's choice of weak, unwilling, and doubting human beings to serve him.

Despite Moses' persistent lack of trust, Yahweh again responds patiently to his objection. He gives Moses three signs. The first makes use of the rod which Moses, because he is a shepherd, carries in his hand. When he casts it on the ground, it becomes a serpent, and when he catches the serpent by the tail, it again becomes a rod. The second involves Moses' hand; when he puts it inside his cloak next to his chest, it comes out in an advanced state of leprosy, and when he repeats the operation, it comes out healthy again. For the third, water taken from the Nile and poured on the ground becomes blood.

As in the story of the burning bush, so in the story of the three signs we are presented with divine activity carried out through such natural phenomena as a snake, leprosy, and river water. Once again, the point of the story lies in Yahweh's use of nature—in this case, to demonstrate his power. The three signs are alike in that they signify the power of God to do ominous things. They differ in that the first two can be and are performed immediately by Moses (and presumably repeated at a later time), while the third can only be promised to Moses, because it must be performed at the Nile in Egypt. All three signs are intended primarily to convince the Israelites to believe and listen to Moses (having been given in response to his protest that they may not do so). But the first sign, especially, also serves as a confirmation and warning to Moses. It is both amusing and appropriate that Moses flees in terror from his rod when it has become a serpent. And the last sign, especially, anticipates the wonders with which Yahweh will smite Egypt (3:20); Egyptians worshipped the Nile and their very life depended on its waters.

What follows Yahweh's presentation of these signs? Incredible though it may seem, what follows is yet another protest from Moses. He makes no mention of the signs that have just been given, but instead returns to the subject of his first protest: his own inadequacy for the task. This time it is his lack of eloquence that he puts forward. There is even a bit of impudence in his comment: "I wasn't eloquent before, and I haven't become eloquent since you spoke to me," is the sense of his words (4:10). Perhaps that is why Yahweh's reply seems more abrupt than the previous ones. Even God's patience wears thin eventually. "Who has made man's mouth?" he asks. "Who makes him dumb, or deaf, or seeing, or blind? Is it not I, the LORD? Now therefore go, and I will be with your mouth and teach you what you shall speak" (4:11-12). Not the eloquence of the speaker, but the presence of God's word, makes the message effective.

We can almost admire Moses' stubbornness: he still has one more protest in him, and he utters it now. He seems to have run out of specific points, and makes a more general request: "Oh, my Lord, send, I pray, some other person" (4:13). The actual words are somewhat less direct than our translation suggests—something like "Please, O Lord, send, I pray, by the hand [of whomever] you will send." This could even be taken as an expression of consent on Moses' part, though not a very enthusiastic one. Yahweh's reply, however, shows that our translation has correctly expressed the intention of Moses' plea. It is another attempt to evade his call, and at last Yahweh is provoked to anger.

Even in his anger, Yahweh shows his patience and generosity. Although he will not release Moses and send someone else

in his place, he will permit Moses to have a helper. Aaron his
brother is a good speaker (a further answer to Moses' fourth
objection) and is very devoted to him. He will serve as his
assistant. But there is no question of Moses' escaping full
responsibility for the mission. Aaron will speak only what
Moses tells him, and Moses will receive his instructions from
Yahweh. There is a reminder to Moses to take with him his
rod (which has already served to teach him a lesson), and with
that Yahweh brings the interview to an end.

The Task Begun

1. The return to Egypt (4:18-31).

That Moses has at last accepted his new vocation can be seen in the next thing he does: he returns to his father-in-law and asks his permission to go back to Egypt. His permission is necessary because Moses, by accepting his hospitality and marrying his daughter, has become part of the family and recognizes the authority of the head of the family.

The reason Moses gives for his request is plausible, but it is not the whole truth. He says that he wishes to return to his kinsmen in Egypt to see whether they are still alive. But he does not tell his father-in-law about Yahweh's appearance to him in the burning bush, or about his call and commission. We can only guess why he is so reticent. Is it because he is embarrassed to speak openly about a profound religious experience? Is it because he is afraid that his claim to have been appointed the deliverer of his people will meet with disbelief and mockery? Or is it because the delicate nature of his mission requires that it be begun in secrecy? Perhaps the context suggests that we have here a last echo of Moses' own reluctance, sense of inadequacy, and doubt as to how he will be received by his own people, once he has returned. In any case, his father-in-law asks for no further explanation, but bids him go in peace.

It may occur to us to wonder what Moses' status will be
when he returns to Egypt. Presumably he had forfeited any
special privilege as the adopted son of Pharaoh's daughter
when he fled to Midian as a fugitive from Egyptian law. But if
he returns, will he not immediately be seized and punished for
his "crime"? We have already been told (2:23) that the Pharaoh of Moses' youth has died. Now Yahweh informs him
that "all the men who were seeking your life are dead" (v. 19).
The coast is clear. Moses takes his family with him back to
Egypt, an indication that he is returning permanently to his
people. He also takes the rod, a token of his obedience to Yahweh's orders. Whatever reservations he may still harbor, he is
committed to the course of action that he has begun.

That course of action, Yahweh next tells Moses, must be
begun by showing Pharaoh the signs that Moses has been
empowered to perform. He is told in advance that this will not
result in Pharaoh's releasing the Israelites. But these preliminary maneuvers all have their place in the divine strategy. In
addition to performing the signs he has been given, Moses is to
deliver a message to Pharaoh that points ahead to the culmination of the struggle between the God of Israel and this great
lord of earthly power: "Thus says the LORD, Israel is my firstborn son, and I say to you, 'Let my son go that he may serve
me'; if you refuse to let him go, behold, I will slay your firstborn son" (vv. 22-23).

This announcement to Pharaoh is to be understood in the
light of the role that Pharaoh plays in the story. As we noted
previously, Pharaoh (himself a god in Egyptian eyes) sets himself up as opponent to Yahweh. His opposition takes the form
of the attempted destruction of Israel. But Israel, we are now
told, has been designated Yahweh's "firstborn son." Pharaoh
must let Israel go; and if he does not, the outcome will be the
death, not of Yahweh's firstborn, but of Pharaoh's. In other
words, in such a contest Yahweh will be the victor!

It is apparently the reference to firstborn sons that provides
a connection with the next episode, which takes place on the

journey from Midian to Egypt and involves a son from Moses' family. The passage (vv. 24-26) is one of the most difficult in the Book of Exodus and, indeed, the whole Bible. The difficulty can be seen in the questions that are left unanswered. One night, when the family has stopped for the night, Yahweh comes and tries to kill him. Who is meant by "him"? Is it Moses? But why should Yahweh seek to kill Moses now? We could understand if that had happened earlier, after four or five of Moses' protests. But now Moses is on his way to Egypt in obedience to Yahweh's word. Is it, then, the child that Yahweh seeks to kill? But no motive is given for such a deed. Then Moses' wife circumcises her son (why is he called "her" son only?). She touches someone's feet with the foreskin (our translation supplies Moses' name, but the original says only "his feet"). Is it Moses or the child who is touched in this way? And what does the touching signify? Next she says (to Moses, or to the child?), "Surely you are a bridegroom of blood to me" (v. 26). As a result, he (presumably Yahweh) leaves him (Moses, or the child?) alone. The episode concludes with a word of explanation: "Then it was that she said, 'You are a bridegroom of blood,' because of the circumcision" (v. 26).

Many attempts have been made to answer the questions raised by this passage, and none has been fully convincing. The best approach to understanding it is to leave aside the insoluble details and ask what the episode adds to the longer story of which it is now part. Before it, Moses sets out with his family for Egypt, where (among other things) he is to warn Pharaoh that disobedience to Yahwah will result in the death of his firstborn son. After it, Moses arrives in Egypt and carries out his commission. The main point of the episode itself is the practice of circumcision, as the concluding word makes clear. This rite appears in the stories about the patriarchs (Gen. 17:9-14), where it is said to provide the required mark of membership in the community God has chosen to be his own. Perhaps what is being said in this passage is that Moses has disobeyed Yahweh by failing to circumcise his son. The penalty for disobedience is no different for Moses than for Pharaoh: the death of the firstborn son. But Moses' wife (the child's mother) acts to head off the judgment: she circumcises her son and marks her husband in such a way as to associate him with her in the act of obedience. Yahweh accepts the circumcision, the threat of judgment is past, and Moses proceeds on his way as an agent obedient to his Master's will. This suggested interpretation by no means answers all the questions, but it serves to make some kind of sense out of the passage in its context.

As Moses nears Egypt, his brother Aaron, prompted by Yahweh, goes out into the wilderness to meet him and welcomes him warmly. It may be significant that this meeting takes place at "the mountain of God" (v. 27), because Moses there gives Aaron a complete report of the commission he received when Yahweh appeared to him. The brothers then go, as instructed (3:16-17), to gather the elders. Aaron speaks the words Moses received from Yahweh. The response of the people confirms the assurance that Yahweh had given to Moses (3:18) and reflects unfavorably on Moses' protest (4:1). They believe, bow their heads, and worship.

2. An unsuccessful interview with Pharaoh (5:1—6:1).

This section is divided into four scenes—the first portrays the interview itself, and the other three the aftermath. We begin with vv. 1-5. According to Yahweh's instructions (3:18), Moses and the elders are to go to the king of Egypt. Aaron is also included as Moses' assistant (4:14-17). Moses and Aaron now proceed to carry this out, but the elders are not specifically mentioned as forming part of the delegation. Possibly this is meant to suggest that they are unwilling to support Moses with their presence. This seems unlikely, however, in view of the enthusiasm with which they have just welcomed him. Probably we are to view the elders too as being present for the interview.

The first words spoken to Pharaoh are at variance with

what Yahweh had instructed. Moses had been told to say,
"The LORD [Yahweh], the God of the Hebrews, has met
with us; and now, we pray you, let us go on a three days' journey into the wilderness, that we may sacrifice to the LORD
our God" (3:18). What Moses and Aaron actually say is,
"Thus says the LORD, the God of Israel, 'Let my people go,
that they may hold a feast to me in the wilderness' " (v. 1).
They begin with the abrupt and unsupported claim to speak
for Yahweh ("Thus says the LORD"); they use the in-group
name for the people ("Israel"), rather than the one familiar to
Pharaoh ("the Hebrews"); they demand ("Let my people go")
rather than request permission to leave; and they specify no
limit on the time they propose to be away. We are not surprised that their arrogant words evoke an equally arrogant reply from the world's most powerful monarch: "Who is the
LORD, that I should heed his voice and let Israel go? I do not
know the LORD, and moreover I will not let Israel go" (v. 2).

Whatever the provocation, these are chilling words. Yet it
is little wonder that Pharaoh has never heard of Yahweh. The
gods of Egypt and of the ancient world in general were closely allied with the monarchies and power-structures of the day.
They supported and guaranteed the political, economic,
social, and religious status quo. With Yahweh it is quite otherwise. Standing outside and apart from the nations and their
rulers, he allies himself with a band of helpless slaves and
demands of the greatest of all monarchs that he set these people free! "Who is the LORD?" is Pharaoh's reply.

Moses and Aaron then moderate their tactics; their next
words are almost exactly those commanded by Yahweh. They
add a phrase, however: "lest he [Yahweh] fall upon us with
pestilence or with the sword" (v. 3). This is probably meant to
provide a motive for their request, or even a motive for Pharaoh to comply with the request, since he would presumably
rather lose a few days' work from his slaves than have them
die. This more respectful approach gains them a less haughty

reply from Pharaoh. Nevertheless, he still refuses their request, saying that it is unacceptable to take the people away from their work.

The second scene (vv. 6-12) involves instructions from Pharaoh to the taskmasters and foremen of the people. He takes punitive action against Israel for the request that has been made. His point of view is that idleness on the part of the Hebrews has led them to seek opportunity to offer sacrifice to their God. So Pharaoh increases their work-load. He requires them to produce as many bricks as before, but rather than continue to provide them with the straw needed as one of the ingredients, he orders them to scrounge for it themselves.

The third scene is portrayed in vv. 13-19. Pharaoh's demands prove unrealistic. The people are unable to maintain their level of production. Thus their Hebrew foremen cannot make delivery, and are beaten by the Egyptian taskmasters. Finally, in desperation, the foremen go to Pharaoh. They do not accuse him of direct responsibility for their hopeless situation, but tell him that the blame belongs to "your own people" (v. 16). He simply repeats his charge, "You are idle, you are idle" (v. 17), and sends them back to work with orders unchanged.

Moses and Aaron are again involved in the final scene (5:20-6:1). Pharaoh's shrewdness has paid off. Once the foremen discover that there is no hope of reversing the new work order, they turn on Moses and Aaron, calling down Yahweh's judgment on them for having brought them into disfavor with Pharaoh, thereby giving him an excuse to oppress them even more. Moses, moreover, reacts to these reproaches by turning on Yahweh, his old spirit of protest reawakened. He had been warned earlier that his mission would not be immediately successful. But he had not known that, as a result of his activity, the circumstances of his people would become so much worse, and that they would hold him responsible. "O LORD, why hast thou done evil to this people?" he cries. "Why didst thou ever send me? For since I came to Pharaoh to speak in thy

name, he has done evil to this people, and thou hast not delivered thy people at all" (vv. 22-23).

Pharaoh has succeeded in sowing dissension in Israel's
ranks. But Yahweh responds to Moses' bitter words neither
with anger nor with explanation. Rather, he turns Moses'
attention to the future, and renews his promise that he will
bring Pharaoh to the point where he will not only let the people go but will virtually drive them out of the country.

3. The call of Moses renewed (6:2—7:7).

The section to which we now turn is in some ways an
enigma. In it we find repeated several of the key elements in
Moses' appointment as leader (3:1—4:17). There is the announcement of the divine name Yahweh; the identification as
God of the patriarchs; the expression of compassion for Israel's plight and the intention to deliver them from bondage and
bring them up to a land of their own; the commissioning of
Moses, followed by his protest; and Yahweh's reply,
including the description of what the outcome will be. There
is even a summary (in the form of a genealogy) of Moses' and
Aaron's family background. All of this is told as if there were
no previous narrative about the preparation and appointment
of Moses as leader or about the initial meetings with the elders
and with Pharaoh.

The probable explanation is that this section records an
account of these events which is parallel to that recorded in
3:1-4:17, but drawn by the author from another source.[1] In the
Book of Exodus, however, it serves as a *renewal* of Moses' call
at a time when he has failed in his first appearance before
Pharaoh, has been reproached by his own people, and has
expressed his disillusionment to Yahweh. Thus to understand
the passage we turn our attention, not to its parallels with the
previous passage, but to what it contributes to the story at this
point.

---

[1]For further explanation of this point, see the discussion of the formation of the
book in the Introduction.

We begin with God's words to Moses in 6:2-8. The central theme is the thrice-repeated announcement, "I am the LORD [Yahweh]" (vv. 2, 6, 8). The repetition indicates that the point of the announcement is not simply to provide information about what Israel should call its God. In any case, the divine name has already been introduced earlier in the narrative (especially 3:15). The point of the announcement is, rather, to set forth the character of this God.

The first announcement, "I am the LORD," is followed by the statement that God appeared to the patriarchs, and established his covenant with them to give them the land of Canaan. This was a beginning, but was not yet a full expression of his character: "by my name the LORD I did not make myself known to them" (v. 3).

The second and third announcements come at the beginning and end of a statement of what God is about to do for Israel. The statement is structured in such a way as to emphasize how fully his character is revealed in the promise. Numbers are often used in the Bible to signal such emphases; threes and sevens are an indication of completeness. It is, therefore, no coincidence that the promise is given in three parts, and that seven phrases declare Yahweh's intention to fulfill it. This can best be seen in an outline of 6:6-8:

> 1. Liberation from Egypt.
>   a) "I will bring you out."
>   b) "I will deliver you."
>   c) "I will redeem you."
>
> 2. Adoption as Yahweh's people.
>   a) "I will take you for my people."
>   b) "I will be your God."
>
> 3. Establishment in the promised land.
>   a) "I will bring you into the land."
>   b) "I will give it to you."

Thus it is above all in what God is about to do for Israel that we can see his character as Yahweh. "I am Yahweh" can here be seen to mean "I am your God": "you shall know that I am the LORD your God" (v. 7).

Moses is reassured by these words, and obeys the divine command to communicate them to the people. But when he does so, he meets with resistance. This is in striking contrast to the response given Moses and Aaron by the elders and the people upon their return to Egypt (4:30-31). Then the people believed and worshiped; now they do not listen. The reason, of course, is the failure of the interview with Pharaoh, made painfully real to the people by the impossible increase in their work load.

Moses' fragile assurance cannot withstand this rejection. When he is next ordered by Yahweh to appear (again) before Pharaoh, with the demand to let the people of Israel go, he resists. He is explicit about his reason: "Behold, the people of Israel have not listened to me; how then shall Pharaoh listen to me?" (6:12). We have already noted Moses' fivefold protest against his call at the burning bush and his outburst against Yahweh after the initial unsuccessful interview with Pharaoh. When we add this further expression of resistance on Moses' part, we have a remarkable picture of timidity and lack of trust on the part of one chosen to play the leading role in Yahweh's deliverance of his people. Once again, however, Yahweh stands firm in holding Moses and Aaron to the task to which they have been appointed. His intentions will not be frustrated just because his people will not listen.

The genealogy which follows marks a point of transition. Moses and Aaron have received "a charge to the people of Israel and to Pharaoh king of Egypt" (6:13). But they have not yet carried it out, despite their initial fruitless effort. The mention of Moses and Aaron just before and just after the genealogy (vv. 13, 26) makes it clear that the intention is to show their family connections. Thus the genealogy begins with the sons of Jacob in the same order in which they appear at the beginning of the book. But it continues only as far as Levi, the third son, since Moses and Aaron are descendants of Levi. The central verse is, therefore, v. 20.

A curious feature of this genealogy, however, is that it records Aaron's wife and descendants (vv. 23, 25), but does not do the same for Moses. This reflects the fact that Aaron was remembered as the ancestor of the priests of Israel, while Moses' descendants play no significant role in subsequent events. The genealogy thus serves the secondary purpose of linking the priesthood to the crucial events of the Exodus, in which Aaron played a part.

Because the genealogy has interrupted the story line, it is followed by a review of events already described, including Yahweh's command, Moses' objection, and the reassurance offered by Yahweh. Near the close of the section, we read that "Moses and Aaron did so; they did as the LORD commanded them" (7:6). There will be times, as the story continues, when Moses (and Aaron even more so!) will act in a manner less than completely pleasing to Yahweh. But there will be no further attempts to evade the basic task. The people of Israel now have a leader and a spokesman.

Struggle with the Enemy

1. A preliminary wonder (7:8-13).

Yahweh now instructs Moses and Aaron about how they are to proceed when they again appear before Pharaoh. On their first appearance, they used only words; this second time, they are to use a sign also. The sign is not to be performed until Pharaoh asks for one. Presumably he will do so because he will be sure that these men will not be able to produce such a thing, and so will be disgraced in the eyes of all, including their own people. That is the point of his challenge: "Prove yourselves by working a miracle" (v. 9). When the time comes, Aaron casts down his rod and it becomes a serpent. This wonder is harmless (if somewhat startling), and is intended to demonstrate the power of Moses and Aaron ("prove *yourselves*") rather than of God. Therefore it is not classed among the plagues, but stands by itself as a prelude to what is to follow.

We are not told whether Pharaoh and his servants are surprised that the two Hebrews are able to work such a miracle. But they are obviously not overwhelmed. Pharaoh summons his own wise men and sorcerers, and they too are able to turn rods into serpents. Aaron's miracle is, to be sure, superior to that of the Egyptians. For one thing, he simply casts his rod down and the rod becomes a serpent (by the power of God, who provided the sign), while the Egyptians have to make use of "their secret arts" (v. 11) for which they were famous in the ancient world. Also, Aaron's rod then swallows up the other rods, in effect nullifying the magicians' accomplishment. But the similarity is sufficient to excuse Pharaoh from attributing any special importance to Moses and Aaron. We are provided with an illustration of the fact that miracles do not impress those who are unwilling to be convinced. So Pharaoh's heart remains hard, and he will not listen.

2. The first nine plagues (7:14—10:29).

Pharaoh's rejection of this sign, which goes hand in hand with his rejection of the word of Yahweh relayed by Moses and Aaron, ushers in a series of plagues on the Egyptians. There are ten of them; the first nine, however, follow one another in sequence, while the tenth is distinguished from the others and represents the culmination of this part of the story. The first nine plagues will be dealt with here, and the tenth reserved for separate treatment.

It will be convenient if we list the first nine plagues at the outset of our discussion, along with the subject of each and the verses in which each is described. They are as follows:

(1) Blood	(4) Flies	(7) Hail
7:14-24	8:20-32	9:13-35
(2) Frogs	(5) Cattle disease	(8) Locusts
7:25-8:15	9:1-7	10:1-20
(3) Gnats	(6) Boils	(9) Darkness
8:16-19	9:8-12	10:21-29

The most obvious feature of these plagues is that they consist of afflictions drawn from the world of nature. Some of them, at least, resemble phenomena known to occur in Egypt from time to time. This is a further instance of a matter we have had occasion to note previously, when we considered the burning bush episode that begins the story of the call of Moses, and the three signs which were given him following his call. The Book of Exodus tells of a God who acts, not *against* nature, but *through* it, because he is Lord of nature.

The plagues are presented as more than mere natural events, of course. Their function in the story does not depend on their absolute uniqueness, however, but on their impact in the context. They happen one after another, apparently in rather rapid succession, at times announced by Yahweh through his spokesman. They are then removed according to Yahweh's command. Their severity is overwhelming, though in specified instances Israel is exempt from their effects. While thus presented as something more than natural calamities, they are also carefully distinguished from products of the magic so widely practiced in the ancient world. This is accomplished by relating how the Egyptian magicians are unable to prevent or remove the plagues. Indeed, they are only able to duplicate the first two, urge Pharaoh to surrender after the third, and are themselves so severely afflicted by the sixth that they are unable even to put in an appearance!

Patterns and variations

At first reading, the passage gives the impression of extreme repetitiveness. This is due in part to the close resemblance of certain plagues: the first is like one of the signs Moses was given to perform before the people, while the third and fourth are very similar to one another. The sense of repetitiveness is also the result of the large number of plagues, and the rather stereotyped formulas with which they are reported.

It is probable that the earlier versions of the story of Israel's deliverance varied somewhat from each other in regard to the plagues which preceded the escape from Egypt. There would have been differences in the way in which the plagues were described, as well as the order in which they were recounted and the total number included (none of them would have had all ten plagues).

The likelihood is, then, that the final author of the Book of

Exodus has combined two or more earlier versions into the plague story as we now have it.[1] No doubt one reason why this was done is simply the desire to preserve all of these treasured memories, so that nothing would be forgotten. But another reason is the opportunity such combining provides for the author to emphasize the meaning of the events. In what follows, we will give our attention to the plague story in its final form.

The pattern followed in describing each of the plagues most frequently contains the following elements:

a) Yahweh instructs Moses concerning the plague.
b) An announcement is made to Pharaoh.
c) The plague occurs.
d) Pharaoh seeks removal of the plague.
e) The plague ends.
f) Pharaoh's heart again becomes hard.

A more careful reading shows, however, that there is greater variety in these accounts than might at first appear. Even the six most common elements, listed above, do not appear in every passage, while there are other elements which appear in some of the passages but not in most of them. Furthermore, there is evidence that the plagues fall into groups or clusters, and that a sequence of events leads toward some climax. Our procedure will be to consider the main themes of the plague narratives, as these emerge from the similarities and differences in the individual episodes. Individual plagues will be referred to by number, 1 through 9, as in the list above.

Each episode opens with Yahweh's instructions to Moses concerning the plague which is to follow. Yahweh initiates each plague in response to Pharaoh's refusal to acknowledge

---

[1]Once again, see the introduction. A similar process can be seen in the traditional Good Friday practice of meditating on "The Seven Last Words of Christ," which do not all appear in any single account but are gathered from all four gospels.

him or let his people go, so that the plagues are the expression and fulfillment of Yahweh's word. Moses makes no further protests to Yahweh; he is now obedient in carrying out his mission.

Moses is usually, but not always, instructed to approach Pharaoh before the plague begins—sometimes when Pharaoh is out-of-doors and sometimes when he is in his palace. There is a pattern in this matter of the approach to Pharaoh which suggests that the narrative may present us with three groups of three plagues each. This can be shown most clearly in a diagram:

P. approached out-of-doors	P. approached in his palace	P. not approached beforehand
1	2	3
4	5	6
7	8	9

Two clarifications are needed. In regard to the first column, Moses is told in 1 and 4 to approach Pharaoh when he goes out to the water (presumably the Nile). In 7, it is not explicitly said that Moses is to find Pharaoh out-of-doors; but the same phrase is used about rising early in the morning, and Moses is told to "stand before Pharaoh," so a setting similar to 1 and 4 seems implied. In regard to the second column, Moses is told to "go in to Pharaoh," which is taken to mean within the palace.

The reason for approaching Pharaoh is, of course, to announce to him in advance the plague that is about to occur. Thus there is such an announcement in the case of six of the nine plagues. As part of the first announcement, Pharaoh's attention is especially called to the rod which is to be used in several of the plagues. As part of the announcement of the seventh plague, he is warned to put his cattle into sheltered places, so that the damage may be moderated. The function of these announcements is to make it clear to Pharaoh that these are no random catastrophes, but the work of Yahweh the God of Israel.

One feature that testifies to the purposefulness of the plagues is that they do not indiscriminately strike all the inhabitants of Egypt. Israel is exempt from the destructive effects of 4, 7, and 9, which do not touch the land of Goshen, where the Israelites live. Also, their cattle are spared in the fifth plague. We are probably to think of Israel being spared in all of them, even where that is not expressly mentioned. More remarkable is the fact that, as a result of advance warning, Egyptians "who feared the word of the LORD" (9:20) are able to take steps to avoid the destruction of plague 7.

It may be that the order in which the plagues occur represents an escalation of their severity. They begin, at any rate, with nuisances and end with death. Certainly the cumulative effect is one of increasingly intolerable suffering. The oppressive weight of the long series of plagues is emphasized by the greater length at which 7, 8, and 9 are narrated. Much of this greater length is devoted to Pharaoh's offers to negotiate and to Yahweh's explanations of the purpose for such a long series of plagues—both matters to which we shall return later.

The action which begins each plague is not always performed by the same person. In the first three plagues, Yahweh instructs Moses to direct Aaron to extend his hand with his rod, and Aaron does so. This seems to provide added support for the possibility that the plagues are arranged in groups of three. In this case, however, the pattern does not hold. Yahweh acts directly in plagues 4 and 5, Moses (with a little help from Aaron) acts in plague 6, and Moses alone acts in the last three of these plagues. What is made clear is that every plague originates solely in Yahweh's command, that Moses is given full responsibility as his spokesman and agent, and that Aaron's position is a completely subordinate one.

In regard to Aaron's role, it is noteworthy that in all the plagues in which he appears, and only in those, the Egyptian magicians also put in an appearance. They succeed in duplicating the first two plagues ("by their secret arts"), but fail in the case of the third and advise Pharaoh that it is "the

finger of God" (8:19); these are the plagues in which Aaron
plays a prominent part. Both Aaron and the magicians have
minor roles in the sixth plague. There is irony in the fact that
the magicians cannot reverse or even halt the calamities, but at
best can only duplicate them. Even when they are
"successful," they only make matters worse! And the humor
becomes broader when, after having been on the sidelines for
some time, they are again mentioned only to report that they
are suffering so badly from the effects of the sixth plague
(boils) that they cannot even put in an appearance. Their failure shows decisively that the plagues fall into an entirely different category than a bag of magic tricks. But why do Aaron
and the magicians always appear together? They are counter-
parts: the magicians are to Pharaoh what Aaron is to Moses
(and Yahweh). They serve as seconds to the principle
adversaries.

The magicians, as we have noted, advise Pharaoh (after they
cannot duplicate the third plague) that it is "the finger of
God." We are not told just what that means, but presumably
they counsel some moderation of Pharaoh's policy. In any
case, he does not pay any attention. This slight hint of division
in the Egyptian ranks finds an echo in two other episodes.
Plague 7 is unique in that, following the announcement of the
coming hail, warning is given to Pharaoh to put his livestock
into shelters. There is no indication that he heeds this warning
himself, but we read: "Then he who feared the word of the
LORD among the servants of Pharaoh made his slaves and his
cattle flee into the houses; but he who did not regard the word
of the LORD left his slaves and his cattle in the field" (9:20-21).
The other episode is plague 8, in which Pharaoh's servants are
finally provoked into a surprisingly bold outburst: "How long
shall this man [Moses] be a snare to us? Let the men go, that
they may serve the LORD their God; do you not yet understand that Egypt is ruined?" (10:7). In the Book of Exodus,
generally speaking, Egypt is simply "the house of bondage"
and Egyptians are the oppressors of Israel, who stand in the

way of God's purpose. But these references show that, even
among those who are by definition God's "enemies," distinctions are possible and necessary.

Indeed, Pharaoh himself is not presented in a totally one-
sided and unsympathetic manner. Although at the end of the
ninth plague he still refuses to give in to Moses' demands, and
has in fact broken off all further contact, he has earlier shown
some flexibility and willingness to negotiate. In more than
half of these nine plagues (2, 4, 7, 8, 9), he offers to make concessions and to compromise. He does so, admittedly, only
when the burden of a catastrophe becomes too heavy to bear,
and he shows a distressing tendency to go back on his word
once the pressure is off. But the real problem, from his point
of view, is that Moses (and ultimately Yahweh) has no intention of compromising and therefore refuses to negotiate.

Pharaoh and his hardness of heart

It was observed earlier that the king of Egypt in the Book of
Exodus is not depicted as just another human being; he is
God's chief opponent, the personification of resistance to the
will of God. His actions are symbolic of all sinfulness, and tell
us something about the biblical understanding of sin. The
sequence in which Pharaoh's responses are pictured in the
plague narrative does not seem to convey anything significant,
but it is possible to see reflected in those varied responses the
outlook which must finally reject Yahweh's demand.

Pharaoh's initial position must surely be that, as divine ruler
of a great world power, he has absolute sovereignty over these
Hebrew aliens in his land. He has an unqualified right to put
them to forced labor or even to put them to death. When confronted with a message from some unknown God who claims
authority over Israel and commands Pharaoh to let Israel go,
Pharaoh can only reject that claim with contempt: "Who is
the LORD, that I should heed his voice and let Israel go? I do
not know the LORD, and moreover I will not let Israel go"
(5:2).

When the claim of this unknown God is supported with a show of power, Pharaoh at first simply ignores it—especially when his magicians are able to duplicate the effects. Eventually, however, those effects become too painful to ignore, and Pharaoh resorts to duplicity to have them reversed. But the pretense that he will give in and meet the demand is already a confession of weakness, and a continuing show of power convinces Pharaoh that he must make some concessions. Those concessions seem to be offered in good faith—let the men go alone; let all the people go but leave the livestock behind—but they are designed to preserve some hold on these people.

When all concessions are utterly rejected, it is apparent that what is being demanded of Pharaoh is unconditional surrender of his sovereignty over Israel. Then, in a rage, he drives Moses out of his presence with the threat of death if he should ever return. He does so in words that remind us of Pharaoh's role as the one who sets himself up as a god in opposition to Yahweh: "Never see my face again," he says to Moses, "for in the day you see my face you shall die" (10:28). This anticipates Yahweh's words to Moses in 33:20: "You cannot see my face; for man shall not see me and live." Yahweh's statement is true; he is in fact the holy God. But Pharaoh's statement is false; he will soon desperately summon Moses to appear before him again, and he will himself be utterly destroyed in his opposition to Yahweh.

Pharaoh's refusal to let Israel go is described, in our story, as a hardening of his heart. This brings us to a matter that has caused readers great difficulty, for several times in the course of the narrative it is said that "the LORD hardened Pharaoh's heart." Inevitably the question arises: does God intervene to prevent repentance and obedience to his will and, if so, can the person thus prevented be held guilty for unrepentance and disobedience?

The first thing to consider in this regard is what is actually said about the hardening of Pharaoh's heart. The first occurrence of the phrase comes after Moses' call and instructions, as he is about to return from Midian to Egypt. In a brief summary of what Moses is to do there, Yahweh warns him, almost parenthetically, of what to expect of Pharaoh: "but I will harden his heart, so that he will not let the people go" (4:21). The second occurrence is virtually a duplicate of the first. It is in the renewal of Moses' call, and is a similar warning about what Pharaoh's attitude will be: "But I will harden Pharaoh's heart, and though I multiply my signs and wonders in the land of Egypt, Pharaoh will not listen to you" (7:3-4). Both of these are summary statements, and concern the outcome (rather than the cause) of a series of events. Their purpose is to prepare Moses for what awaits him in Egypt.

It is important to go on to the actual description of the events, given in the plague narratives themselves. We find, when we do so, that the hardening of Pharaoh's heart is spoken of in other ways as well. In connection with three of the plagues (2, 4, 7), Pharaoh is said to harden his own heart (8:15; 8:32; 9:34). In connection with another three plagues (1, 3, 5), it is simply reported that his heart was hard, without reference to how that came about (7:14; 8:19; 9:7).[2] The same neutral expression also appears at the end of the preliminary wonder (7:13), as it does in plague 7, side by side with the statement that Pharaoh hardened his own heart (9:35).

Thus in the first five plagues there is no suggestion that Pharaoh's repeated refusal to obey Yahweh's word is anything but his own freely-chosen act. Even in the seventh plague, his decision is said to be his own. Only in connection with plagues 6, 8, and 9 do we find reference to Yahweh hardening Pharaoh's heart (9:12; 10:20; 10:27; it is also found in 11:10 in the episode of the tenth plague, which we shall consider below).

[2]In the case of this phrase, our translation leaves the door open to misunderstanding. It reads, in each instance, "Pharaoh's heart was hardened"—which suggests a hardening by some outward agent, presumably Yahweh. But the original simply says that Pharaoh's heart *was hard*, a neutral statement which does not place responsibility anywhere outside Pharaoh himself.

What are we to conclude, then, about the hardening of Pharaoh's heart? Perhaps we are simply presented with three different ways of saying the same thing: Pharaoh hardened his heart; Pharaoh's heart was hard; Yahweh hardened Pharaoh's heart. That would be consistent with Israel's belief in the ulti-mate sovereignty of Yahweh, who turns all the deeds of per-sons and nations to his own account. Sometimes one speaks of intermediate causes, and sometimes not, but in the final analy-sis everything is of God.

If, however, the phrases are intended to specify different sources for Pharaoh's hardness of heart, then perhaps we are being told that there comes a point at which freely-chosen acts of sin and rebelliousness become a pattern of behavior from which we cannot choose to escape. What begins as defiance against God ends as judgment by God. This is a harsh truth, but it is consistent with biblical teaching generally (consider, for example, Isa. 6:9-13 and Rom. 1:18-32). Certainly the fig-ure of Pharaoh in the Book of Exodus is of one who has set himself up as the great opponent of Yahweh who, for genera-tion after generation, oppresses, enslaves, and destroys Yah-weh's people. Whatever the purpose of the plagues may be, they are not punishment for an innocent monarch being help-lessly manipulated by an arbitrary deity.

We do well, however, to keep these few phrases in perspec-tive. The passage is not intended as an essay on the theological and philosophical issue of human freedom and divine deter-minism. They appear in the context of a series of plagues, signs that mark the beginning of Yahweh's promised deliverance from a brutal tyrant and nation, who will not acknowledge Yahweh's sovereignty and who exhibit tenacious resistance to his will.

Purpose of the plagues

We turn, then, to a consideration of the purpose of the plagues. In the majority of references which bear on this point, they are said to take place for the sake of their effect on Pharaoh and the Egyptians. This does not mean, however, that their purpose is punishment. It is true that they are all calamities of one sort or another, and so imply the judgment of Yahweh on those who oppress his people and resist his will. But if punishment were their only or primary purpose, it could only be asked why the process should be so prolonged and why so many ineffectual measures should be taken. Surely God can execute his judgment more efficiently than this!

In fact, however, it is never stated that the purpose of the plagues is punishment. Rather, it is repeatedly said that they take place so that Pharaoh and the Egyptians may "know." This theme is already established in the initial interview of Moses and Aaron with Pharaoh; as a result of the deliverance of Israel, "the Egyptians shall know that I am the LORD" (7:5). The same general point recurs in connection with specific plagues (1, 2, 4, 7), with slight variations but always following the phrase "that you may know": "that I am the LORD"; "that there is no one like the LORD our God"; "that I am the LORD in the midst of the earth"; "that there is none like me in all the earth"; and "that the earth is the LORD's" (7:17; 8:10, 22; 9:14, 16, 29). It is not always the onslaught of the plague which "shows" this; sometimes it is the lifting of the plague (2, 7), and once it is the exemption of the land of Goshen (where the people of Israel live) from the plague (4).

In one instance, it is said that these things take place so that *Israel* "may know that I am the LORD" (plague 8; 10:2), and is related to the passing along of the story from one generation to another. This picks up a theme which appeared earlier. When Moses was instructed in the changing of his rod into a serpent, he was told that its purpose was that Israel "may believe that the LORD . . . has appeared to you" (4:5). And in the renewal of his call he was instructed to tell Israel that their deliverance from Egypt was so that "you shall know that I am the LORD your God" (6:7). There is also one instance in which the power of Yahweh, exhibited in the full number of plagues, has a more universal outreach: "so that my name may be declared throughout all the earth" (9:16).

The purpose of the plagues, then, is to serve as *signs*. What is *significant* about them is that they point to the presence and activity and power of Yahweh, both to judge and to deliver. These signs are provided so that Yahweh may be known. They are given primarily for Pharaoh and the Egyptians. Pharaoh had said to Moses and Aaron at that initial, unsuccessful interview, "Who is the LORD, that I should heed his voice and let Israel go? I do not know the LORD, and moreover I will not let Israel go" (5:2). By the time the plagues have all taken place, despite repeated hardening of heart, Pharaoh has acknowledged Yahweh and sent Israel on its way. The signs are given also for Israel and for the whole world, that Jews and Gentiles alike may acknowledge and obey this God.

3. The tenth plague (11; 12:29-42).

This plague is distinguished from the others in a number of ways. Each of the nine plagues thus far has involved Moses and Aaron in one or more audiences with Pharaoh. The conversations were sometimes acrimonious, but further audiences were not precluded. Following the ninth plague, however, a new note enters. Pharaoh makes what must seem to him a last, generous concession. Moses responds with an unbudging refusal. Pharaoh then orders Moses out of his presence, and forbids him to return under the threat of death. Moses agrees that he will not return. Clearly a new stage has been reached in the story.

Furthermore, Yahweh announces the tenth plague to Moses with the assurance that it will be the last, and that after it Pharaoh will not only let the Israelites go but will drive them away. In view of their imminent departure, they are to collect valuables from their Egyptian neighbors, as Moses had previously been told that they would do (3:21-22).

The opening sentences of Exodus 11 (vv. 1-3) interrupt the

sequence of events. Moses has just responded, at the end of chapter 10, to Pharaoh's strong prohibition of any further interviews by agreeing that he would not return. But in 11:4-9 Moses is announcing the tenth plague to Pharaoh, with no explanation of how a further interview might have been arranged. It seems best to think of what is described in 11:4-9 as following immediately after chapter 10, and as constituting the rest of Moses' angry speech to an equally angry Pharaoh. Why, then, has 11:1-3 been inserted into the story here? As we have seen, it precedes the announcement of the tenth plague in order to mark it off as the final and decisive one.

Also, between the announcement of this plague (in chapter 11) and its occurrence (in 12:29-42) come two further interruptions in the sequence. The first is the summary statement in 11:10. Even though the tenth plague has yet to take place, Moses and Aaron will have no more to say to Pharaoh. From now on, their attention will be directed to the people of Israel. The other interruption concerns the preparation of the feast which would mark Israel's deliverance from bondage. The passage in which this preparation is set forth will be discussed in our next section. We note it here as one further indication that the tenth plague is distinguished from the other nine. It marks the culmination of the plagues, but also points ahead to the next period in the life of Yahweh's people.

The tenth plague unfolds as Moses had announced. All the Egyptian firstborn, from Pharaoh's family down to the family of the lowliest captive, and including even domestic animals, die at midnight. There is a great outcry, and at long last it does not come from the oppressed Israelites, but from those who for so long oppressed them. Pharaoh's reaction is dramatic. He summons Moses and Aaron, thus reversing his angry insistence that they were never to see him again; in his extreme agitation, he does so in the middle of the night. He tells them to leave the country, along with all the people of Israel. Abandoning his last hold over them, he tells them to take along their flocks and their herds. As a mark of his total capitulation, he twice uses the phrase, "As you have said." Most striking of all, this proud figure who had mockingly asked, "Who is the LORD?" now in his surrender begs, "And bless me also!" (12:32).

The Egyptians, afraid for their lives, join their king in urging the Israelites to leave quickly. The Israelites do so, setting off in such haste that they take with them no provisions except dough that was not leavened. They already have the objects they had requested from their Egyptian neighbors, however, and do not leave those behind.

So the people of Israel begin their journey. They set off from Rameses. Apparently this is the same place as the second of the two store cities which, according to 1:11, they built for Pharaoh; it represents the intolerable slavery which they now leave behind. They travel first as far as Succoth (the location of which is not known for certain). They are said to number 600,000 men, along with women and children—not to mention hangers-on and a large quantity of livestock. This is far too enormous a number to be taken literally, either for the Israelite population in the Nile delta or for their coming stay in the wilderness. Since the number is simply mentioned in passing, and not in connection with some great divine wonder, we should probably view it as intended to impress on our minds the great increase in this family since the day when 70 members of Jacob's household came to settle in Egypt. In addition, it is a way of suggesting that the deliverance of Yahweh is experienced not only by those who were literally present at the exodus event, but by all Israelites of every generation. That they are accompanied by a "mixed multitude" (12:38) may also hint at the significance of this event for those who are not actually part of the community of Israel. It has been a long sojourn (this passage says 430 years), and the people keep vigil on the night of their departure. Such a night of watching is to be kept by their descendants in memory of the deliverance from Egypt.

Commemorations of the Event

1. Passover and unleavened bread (12:1-28).

We turn now to three closely-related passages (12:1-28; 12:43-51; 13:1-16) which involve the observance of the passover, the feast of unleavened bread, and the consecration of the firstborn. The passages provide later generations with rather detailed instructions for commemorating the deliverance from Egypt. These instructions are placed in the context of the events which are to be commemorated.

We have already seen that the first of these three passages is placed before the report of the tenth plague in order to set that plague apart from the nine which have gone before. The passage itself begins with instructions given by Yahweh to Moses and Aaron (vv. 1-20), continues with a speech by Moses to the elders and the people (vv. 21-27), and ends with a brief report of the people's response (v. 28).

The first part of the instructions has to do with "the LORD's passover" (v. 11). The month which sees Israel's departure from Egypt is designated the first month of the year, since it is the month in which Israel begins life anew. The whole congregation of Israel is to take part in the feast which is prescribed, because the whole community is involved in what is being celebrated. Yahweh's deliverance is a collective one. The celebration is to take place, however, in family units.

Each family is to take a lamb (or if the families are small, two may share a lamb). The lamb is to be unblemished, a one-year-old male, and is to be kept separate from the rest of the flock from the tenth of the month (when it is selected) until the fourteenth (which is the eve of Israel's departure).

On that evening, all are to kill their lambs, taking some of the blood and putting it on the doorposts and lintels of their houses. Then they are to roast the lambs and eat the meat with unleavened bread and bitter herbs. The meat must be prepared in the prescribed way, and any that is left over must be burned. The meal is to be eaten in haste, with the participants dressed for immediate departure.

Up to this point, no explanation has been given for the feast or its various components. But now it is announced as the ceremony marking the night in which Yahweh will bring about the tenth plague: "It is the LORD's passover. For I will pass through the land of Egypt that night, and I will smite all the firstborn in the land of Egypt, both man and beast; and on all the gods of Egypt I will execute judgments: I am the LORD" (12:11-12).

The only individual feature given a specific explanation is the blood put on the entrances of the houses. It is a sign that Yahweh will "pass over" the homes of the Israelites and spare them the deaths of their firstborn. Note that the blood is not a sign for Yahweh, as if he would not know which houses to skip if they were left unmarked! It is a sign "for you"—that is, for Israel—of the protecting and delivering grace of their God.

The other part of Yahweh's instructions concerns the feast of unleavened bread. For seven days the people are to eat bread which has been made without yeast or other leavening agents. On the first day, all such ingredients are to be removed from their houses. The first and seventh days are to be days on which no one is to work; rather, a "holy assembly" is to be held on each of them. No reason is given for prohibiting bread that has been leavened, but the first day of the feast is iden tified with the eve of the passover. The entire observance is associated with the liberation of Israel from bondage: "And you shall observe the feast of unleavened bread, for on this very day I brought your hosts out of the land of Egypt" (v. 17).

Moses' speech to the elders and people, which follows, mentions only the passover and not the feast of unleavened bread. Even the words about the passover do not simply repeat Yahweh's instructions, but omit many items and add some others, such as the use of a bunch of hyssop to apply the blood to the entrance, and the requirement to stay inside the house for the entire night. What is most notable about this speech is the emphasis on future observance. Yahweh's instructions already contained this element: "This day shall be for you a memorial day, and you shall keep it as a feast to the LORD; throughout your generations you shall observe it as an ordinance for ever" (v. 14; see also v. 17). Now the requirement is repeated, even specifying how it is to be explained to the children: "And when your children say to you, 'What do you mean by this service?' you shall say, 'It is the sacrifice of the LORD's passover' " (vv. 26-27).

This emphasis on future observance reminds us of what we noted in the Introduction about the character of the Book of Exodus. It is the culmination of a long tradition in which the story of Yahweh's saving activity was recited in the context of worship and for the purpose of strengthening the worshipers' faith. The passages about Israel's celebration of its deliverance are not intended to describe how the generation that participated in the escape from Egypt celebrated the event. Rather, they seek to involve every Israelite in that great deliverance. These acts of commemoration make the exodus an ever-present event for every generation.

Concerning the people's response, we are told only that they worshiped and obeyed. Just as Moses' initial reluctance and protests were overcome, so (thanks apparently to the plagues) have been those of the people—at least for the time being. Their observance of the passover and the feast of unleavened bread then leads into the narrative about the carrying out of the last plague and the beginning of Israel's journey.

2. More about the passover (12:43-51).

This passage, like the previous one, begins with instructions from Yahweh to Moses and Aaron, and ends with a report of the people's obedience. It does not contain a speech by Moses to the people, although it is of course implied that the instructions were communicated.

The instructions again assume the conditions of a later era. This time they concern primarily the question of who may eat the passover. Generally speaking, no non-Israelites may do so. It is a feast in which the people of Yahweh commemorate their experience of deliverance; it would be inappropriate for those who have not shared the experience to take part in the feast. But provisions are made here to avoid an unwarranted exclusivism. They are somewhat confusing, but may be understood to say that purchased slaves and resident aliens are to be included in the observance, providing they are circumcised—providing, that is, that they associate themselves with the community and become part of it. The summary statement which follows is an important testimony to the attitude Israel is to have in these matters: "There shall be one law for the native and for the stranger who sojourns among you" (v. 49). Again the people are said to respond in obedience, and this is followed by a reference to Yahweh's bringing the people out of Egypt "on that very day" (v. 51).

3. Firstlings and more about unleavened bread (13:1-16).

The arrangement of this section is similar to that of the previous two. First, very briefly this time, are the divine instructions to Moses (vv. 1-2). Next is Moses' speech to the people (vv. 3-16). There is, however, no report here of how the people respond.

Yahweh's instructions mention only the requirement to consecrate to him all of the firstborn. Moses' speech begins by describing, in some detail, how the feast of unleavened bread is to be kept after Israel has entered the promised land. Again it is associated with liberation from bondage, and again there is reference to the explanation to be given to the son who inquires about it.

Only then does Moses turn to the subject of "firstlings." Detailed instructions are given as to how the consecration is to be carried out. It is set in the context of Israel's life after it receives the land. Every firstborn creature belongs to Yahweh and is to be "set apart" to him. Generally this means that it is to be offered up as a sacrifice; this is in fact the procedure to be followed with those animals suitable for sacrifice, such as sheep, goats, and cattle. Those not suitable, such as asses, are either to be killed (but not as a sacrifice) or "redeemed" by a substitute sacrifice. Human firstborn are not to be sacrificed or killed, of course, but similarly redeemed (an example of this is the presentation of the infant Jesus in the temple, Luke 2:22-24). Once more an answer is provided for the son who asks the meaning of the observance. This time it is linked with both deliverance from bondage and the tenth plague. The association with the latter is a natural one, since the plague involved the death of the Egyptian firstborn.

We may summarize by noting that three distinct observances are drawn together as commemorations of Israel's deliverance. They are the passover, the feast of unleavened bread, and the consecration of the firstborn. Whatever may have been the origin and original significance of each of these, they are now presented in relation to the events of the exodus, the manner of their observance after entering the promised land, and the explanation of them to be offered to succeeding generations. These presentations are not sharply divided from each other, but the main emphases are distributed in the following way:

	passover	unleavened bread	firstlings
relation to the event	12:1-13, 21-24	12:14-20; 13:3-4	13:1-2
observance in the land	12:25, 43-49	13:5-7	13:11-13
explanation to posterity	12:26-27	13:8-10	13:14-16

It is significant that all three items are held together in these passages. We are not given a precise, objective account of the historical circumstances surrounding Israel's departure from Egypt, apart from the way in which it was celebrated by and interpreted to later generations. Also, we are not given some bare instructions regarding dietary practices, sacrifices, and the like, apart from the memories and meanings that lie behind them. Again, we do not have an abstract discussion of deliverance as a theological concept, apart from God's concrete acts of deliverance and his people's response in worship. Event, observance, and explanation are inseparably bound together in the biblical witness.

It is also significant that these passages look both to the past and to the future. They recall Yahweh's powerful deliverance of his people in the days of Moses and they anticipate his gift of a land in which his people will flourish. Every generation of God's people lives between memory and hope, between remembrance of what God has done in times past and anticipation of what he will do in times to come. Every generation needs the promise which is both "to deliver them out of the hand of the Egyptians" and "to bring them up out of that land to a good and broad land, a land flowing with milk and honey" (3:8).

The Great Deliverance

1. The departure of Israel (13:17—14:4).

We come now to the heart of our story (the very name by which we call this book—"Exodus"—means "departure, the way out"). The people have already begun their movement within Egypt (12:37), and soon they will cross the border.

The most direct route to Canaan, the land of promise, would be "the way of the land of the Philistines" (13:17), running northeast from the Nile delta along the coast of the Mediterranean Sea. We are told, however, that God does not lead them that way. He leads them, rather, by "the way of the wilderness toward the Red Sea" (13:18).[1] Two reasons are given for this more indirect route. The first is God's private reason, so to speak. The way of the Philistines is the major highway into Egypt from the north and east, and so is heavily fortified. It is likely that the people, confronted with a show of military might, will change their minds and turn back. The second reason, which Yahweh announces to Moses, is that, when Israel takes the way of the wilderness, Pharaoh will be misled into thinking that the people are lost and trapped, and will be tempted to pursue them. This will suit Yahweh's

---

[1]The name "Red Sea" in our translation is somewhat misleading, since it may be taken to refer to the large body of water between Africa and the Arabian peninsula, which bears that name. In the original, the name actually means "Reed Sea" or "Sea of Reeds," and is probably to be understood to refer to a body of water in the marshy region through which the Suez Canal now runs.

purposes, because it will be the occasion for him to "get glory over Pharaoh," so that "the Egyptians shall know that I am the LORD" (14:4). Thus the coming victory over the pursuing army will serve the same purpose as the plagues, but in an even greater and more decisive way. It should be noted that this is not a matter of compelling Pharaoh to do what he does not want to do. Rather, Pharaoh is given opportunity to follow his chosen course, so that the power and purpose of Yahweh may be clearly demonstrated.

As the people begin their journey, Moses brings the bones of Joseph with him. This takes us back to the beginnings of Israel's stay in Egypt. It was Joseph who was responsible for bringing his father and brothers and their households to Egypt. But it was remembered that this was not to be a permanent settlement; Joseph had asked that, when God came to take his family out of Egypt, they would take his bones with them.

The narrative emphasizes Yahweh's leadership of his people and his constant presence in their midst. His presence takes the form, for the most part, of a pillar of cloud by day and a pillar of fire by night, guiding and protecting Israel. This picks up the symbolism, already noted in connection with the burning bush, of God's presence marked by fire (and also by cloud or smoke; note the call of the prophet Isaiah in Isaiah 6 and the ascension of Jesus in Acts 1).

The exact route taken by Israel as they leave Egypt, like that which they follow in the wilderness, can no longer be traced. It is sufficient to note that, as they make their round-about way toward the border, they camp at a place beside the sea. It is there that Yahweh's great victory over the opposing forces is won.

2. The Egyptian pursuit (14:5-18).

Beginning with the coming of the tenth plague, Pharaoh has been portrayed as willing—indeed, eager—for Israel to depart. When he is told, however, that they have actually done so, he reverts to the behavior that followed the other plagues. He and his servants change their minds and regret the loss of their slaves. So Pharaoh mobilizes his armed forces (considerable emphasis is placed on their size and strength, and especially the presence of many chariots), and pursues them. There is again a reference to Yahweh hardening Pharaoh's heart.

The Egyptian army overtakes the Israelites while they are camped by the sea. Understandably, the Israelites are frightened and cry out to Yahweh. They also seek someone near at hand to blame, and turn on Moses as the one most obviously responsible for their plight. In words reminiscent of those spoken by their foreman to Moses and Aaron, when Pharaoh increased the workload of the Israelites (5:21), they complain bitterly about their impending death. They remind him that they were reluctant to follow him: "Is not this what we said to you in Egypt, 'Let us alone and let us serve the Egyptians'?" (v. 12). They would rather have continued as slaves than face what seems to be certain destruction.

Moses does not answer them directly. Showing no traces of his own earlier fears, doubts, and protests, he urges them to be courageous and to rely on Yahweh. They are terrified because they do not see any way to save themselves. But it is not a matter of the Israelites saving themselves—even with the help of Yahweh. The battle is Yahweh's alone. No human effort is needed. Moses summons Israel to the most radical kind of trust. "The LORD will fight for you, and you have only to be still" (v. 14).

Yahweh then speaks to Moses. His opening words suggest that Moses may not have been quite so brave in private as he was in public. "Why do you cry to me?" he asks Moses (v. 15). Then he instructs him about what he is to do. He is to tell the people of Israel to go forward, and then lift up his rod and stretch out his hand over the sea to divide it, so that the people of Israel may go through. Moses is also told that the Egyptians will continue to pursue them, and it is again said that this will be the means for getting glory over the Egyptians and showing them that he is Yahweh.

3. Yahweh's victory (14:19-31).

The divine activity begins with a period of protection against the immediate onslaught of the Egyptian forces. "The angel of God" (that is, God's visible manifestation), accompanied by the pillar of cloud, moves between the Egyptians and the Israelites. This keeps them apart through the night, while the sea is prepared for Israel's crossing.

The manner in which that crossing takes place is not completely clear. As the story now stands, Moses stretches out his hand over the sea, and Yahweh sends a strong east wind which blows all night, making the sea dry land and dividing the waters. The people of Israel then proceed to cross the sea, walking on dry ground, while the waters stand like walls on either side of them. The Egyptians pursue them into the sea, but are "discomfited" by Yahweh; their chariot wheels become clogged, and they try to flee. Yahweh then instructs Moses to stretch out his hand again over the sea, and the result is that the waters return to their normal position. The Egyptians, curiously enough, flee *into* the sea and are "routed." The waters return and cover the entire Egyptian army, and Israel sees the Egyptians dead on the seashore.

It is evident in this account that Israel has passed a major barrier and escaped the forces of the oppressor. But the lack of clarity concerning the details of the event is a reminder that the biblical author is working with traditional materials which sometimes resist simple combination. In fact, this whole passage (13:17—14:31) provides an especially good example of the way in which the biblical author makes use of the sources available to him. He weaves them together with great artistry, but is not concerned to remove all discrepancies. He thus leaves us the clues for recovering, with a high degree of probability, the separate versions of Israel's earlier recitals of the story. We shall use this example to illustrate what was said in the Introduction about the formation of the Book of Exodus.

A brief review of the inconsistencies in the passage will point the way.

a) According to 13:17, "Pharaoh let the people go"; according to 14:5, he "was told that the people had fled."

b) The deity is sometimes referred to as "God" (13:17, etc.) and sometimes as "the LORD" (*Yahweh*) (13:21, etc.).

c) When God does not deal directly with the people, his presence is sometimes said to be "by day in a pillar of cloud . . . and by night in a pillar of fire" (13:21, etc.), but also to take the form of "an angel of God" (14:19).

d) Two reasons are given for the people not taking the most direct route to the promised land: "Lest the people repent when they see war, and return to Egypt" (13:17); and "Pharaoh will say of the people of Israel, 'They are entangled in the land; the wilderness has shut them in'" (14:3).

e) The sea is divided by Moses' "rod" and/or "hand" (14:16, 21, 26); it is also driven back "by a strong east wind" (14:21).

f) The Egyptians are said to be defeated because their chariots get stuck in the mud (14:21); they are also said to drive into the sea (presumably on dry ground, 14:22, 29), only to be overwhelmed and drowned when the walls of water collapse over them (14:28).

It is on the basis of clues like this (not only in this passage, of course, but throughout the Pentateuch) that it is possible to distinguish among the sources used by the biblical author. These sources are described in general terms in the Introduction. So far as this passage is concerned, we may identify the contributions of the various earlier versions as follows.[2]

The Yahwistic source (J). Pharaoh is told that the people have fled. The deity is regularly referred to as "the LORD" (Yahweh). He is present with Israel in a pillar of cloud and fire. No reference is made to the people leaving by an indirect route. The sea is driven back by a strong east wind. And the Egyptians are defeated in a battle from which they flee into the sea.

The Priestly source (P). No reference is made to whether the people left with Pharaoh's permission or without his knowledge. Here, too, as in J, the deity is regularly referred to as "the LORD." He is apparently to be thought of as dealing immediately with the people, since no mention is made of either pillar or angel. The people are commanded to take an indirect route in order to mislead Pharaoh. The sea is divided when Moses stretches out his hand. Finally, the Egyptians drive on dry ground into the midst of the sea and are drowned when the walls of water collapse.

The Elohistic source (E). This source is present in this passage only in fragmentary form; a few scholars maintain that it does not appear here at all. Most, however, would ascribe certain features to E. Pharaoh gave the people permission to leave. The deity is regularly referred to as "God." He is present with his people as an angel. He leads the people on an indirect route in order to avoid war. Moses is said to use a rod in dealing with the sea. And the wheels of the Egyptian chariots become clogged.

There are, therefore, distinctive elements in the earlier versions of the story, and these have been retained by the biblical author (at the cost of some inconsistency) as he has woven

[2]For a verse-by-verse analysis of the passage into the sources, consult the works listed in the Bibliography. Although the analyses by various scholars may differ in specific details, there is general agreement about the contents of the main sources.

them into a single narrative. This is likely to be disturbing to a person who wishes to know exactly "what happened." The fact is that we cannot reconstruct, from the biblical witness, the precise details of the historical event, although the broad outline is certainly there.

Neither the biblical author nor those who told the story before him were concerned to convey bare information about the event. Each version, including the final one, sets forth the event in such a way as to proclaim its meaning and significance for the people of God. The narrative we have before us testifies that Yahweh has won the victory. A helpless, enslaved people has been set free. All the might of a great world power has been destroyed. The arch-enemy of Yahweh, the "god" Pharaoh, has been brought down to defeat. Yahweh is victorious.

The sequel to the event is a changed attitude on Israel's part. Before the crossing, they were in great fear of Pharaoh and the Egyptians; now "the people feared the LORD." They had cried out to Yahweh and complained to Moses; now "they believed in the LORD and in his servant Moses" (v. 31). The Egyptian bondage is over, and Israel is on its way, on the threshold of a new life of freedom.

4. The celebration (15:1-21).

So far, the Book of Exodus has consisted entirely of prose narrative. Now, for the first time, we are presented with some sections of poetry, and appropriately so, for the response of God's people to their deliverance calls for more than prosaic discussion. We were told, at the end of the previous section, that the people feared and believed in Yahweh. In what follows, they give expression to their awe and faith.

This section consists of two songs, one long (vv. 1-18), the other short (v. 21). The introduction to the first song ascribes it to Moses and the people of Israel. We must not understand this too narrowly, for the song begins with references to the crossing of the sea, but goes on to celebrate events that still lie ahead (including some which will take place only after Moses and that whole generation are long dead). It is a song which the later people of Israel sing as they remember all Yahweh's acts of deliverance, beginning with the victory at the sea.

The song itself opens with words which assert that God's powerful deeds have aroused the gratitude of his people, who break into hymns because they are the beneficiaries of his grace:

"I will sing to the LORD, for he has triumphed gloriously; the horse and his rider he has thrown into the sea.

"The LORD is my strength and my song, and he has become my salvation; this is my God, and I will praise him, my father's God, and I will exalt him" (15:1-2).

The song is constructed around several of Yahweh's great victories, in which he delivered his people from the enemy. The most prominent of these is, as we might expect, the deliverance at the Sea of Reeds (vv. 4-5, 8-10, 12). But there are also allusions to Israel's safe passage through the wilderness (v. 13), the overcoming of enemy people (vv. 14-16), the settlement in the land and perhaps even the establishment of the temple in Jerusalem (v. 17). Along with these are more general statements about the kind of God Yahweh has shown himself to be (vv. 3, 6-7, 11, 18). The song concludes with an affirmation of God's kingly rule, which is expressed in all his acts and in all his attributes: "The Lord will reign for ever and ever" (v. 18).

The shorter of the two songs is ascribed to Miriam and the women. Miriam is identified as "the prophetess." Aaron was earlier said to be Moses' prophet (7:1), in a context in which he was designated as the one who would speak for Moses. Here, then, Miriam is being identified as the spokeswoman. She is called "the sister of Aaron." That would also make her Moses' sister, but perhaps Aaron is mentioned here because he was the older brother. In any case, Miriam and Aaron share a second-ary place, assisting the brother to whom Yahweh has given the leadership of Israel.

Miriam and the women accompany their song with dancing and the sound of timbrels (a sort of tambourine). This seems to have been the accepted way to celebrate a victory; on a later occasion, a leader of Israel named Jephthah wins a victory over the enemy Ammonites and, when he returns home, "his daughter came out to meet him with timbrels and with dances" (Judg. 11:34). The words of Miriam's song are the same as the opening words of the first song. The greater length of that first song, and its references to later events in Is-rael's history, suggest that it developed out of Miriam's song as future generations continued to celebrate Yahweh's victories.

It is noteworthy that it is Yahweh, and Yahweh alone, who is praised for the great deliverance. In the preceding prose section, Moses is given a prominent role in the victory, and the people, according to the concluding words, "believed in the LORD and in his servant Moses" (14:31). But even there the victory is called "the great work which the LORD did," and it is Yahweh whom "the people feared." Now, in these songs, Yahweh stands alone as Deliverer; the only role given to Mo-ses and Miriam is to lead the people in celebration. It is as Mo-ses told the fearful people beside the sea: "The LORD will fight for you, and you have only to be still" (14:14).

After Deliverance,
Then What?

1. Bitter water made sweet (15:22-27).

With the crossing of the Sea of Reeds and the destruction of the pursuers, Israel is at last free of Egyptian bondage and has nothing more to fear from that quarter. Now begins the long period of wandering in the wilderness (40 years is the round number given in the biblical story), which provides the setting not only for the rest of the Book of Exodus, but for all that follows until the entrance into the land, the subject of the Book of Joshua.

Israel travels from the Sea of Reeds into the wilderness of Shur, and arrives at a place called Marah. These sites cannot be positively identified, but it is clear that the Israelites are not wandering aimlessly, because it is said that Moses leads them on their way. The journey, begun in such exultation, soon takes on a somber character. After travelling for several days (three is another biblical round number) without water, the people find that the water of Marah suits the name of the place. The word "Marah" means "bitter," and the water is, in fact, undrinkable.

The reaction of the people is surprising, in light of their exuberant celebration following the deliverance at the sea. Their disappointment is understandable, however, when they find themselves deep in the desert and without drinkable

water. "And the people murmured against Moses, saying,
'What shall we drink?'" (v. 24). This rebellious attitude was
already anticipated in the words of the Hebrew foremen who
were faced with impossible demands (5:19-21) and of the Israelites who thought that they were trapped between the Egyptian army and the Sea of Reeds (14:10-12). It will surface many
more times, and is one of the major motifs of the wilderness
narratives.

Moses responds to the murmuring by crying to Yahweh,
who promptly provides a remedy. He shows Moses a tree
which, when thrown into the water, makes it fit to drink.
Then, still at Marah, the people are given a statute and an
ordinance, and are also "proved" or tested. The meaning of the
passage is not very clear, but it seems likely that the people
have been tested by the lack of water, to see whether they
would trust Yahweh and the leader he had provided. The statute and ordinance would then be the announcement that, from
this time on, the people of Yahweh must do his will if they are
to escape the same judgment that fell on the enemy. If they
obey, they will find that Yahweh is not their destroyer but
their healer. The people then move on to an oasis called Elim,
where there is abundant water and vegetation.

2. Quails and manna for food (16:1-36).

After a time, the people continue their journey. We are not
told how long they stayed at Marah or Elim, but more than a
month had passed since they left Egypt by the time they
reached the spot where the episode described in this chapter
takes place. That spot is "between Elim and Sinai" (v. 1), an
indication that they are on their way to Sinai before
continuing on to the promised land. The region is called "the
wilderness of Sin" ("Sin" is a proper name, of course, and has
nothing to do with the English word "sin"—though, as it
happens, the people *do* sin there!).

At Marah, the people had murmured for water; now they

murmur for food. As before, their complaints are directed against Moses (and Aaron), and take the form of wishing that they were back in Egypt—a wish similar to that which they had expressed before their deliverance at the sea (14:11-12). "Would that we had died by the hand of the LORD in the land of Egypt," they say, "when we sat by the fleshpots and ate bread to the full; for you have brought us out into this wilderness to kill this whole assembly with hunger" (v. 3).

Three things suggest that Israel's complaint this time is more blameworthy than their complaint at Marah. First, they might be expected to have learned something from Yahweh's provision of good water at Marah, and from the warning that followed. Second, there is no indication in this passage that they are in genuine need of food, as they were of water at Marah. And finally, their recollection of their circumstances in Egypt is faulty; in the ancient Near East, meat would very seldom have been part of the diet of ordinary men and women, much less of an oppressed group of slaves. Their reference to sitting by the "fleshpots" and eating their fill of bread represents an unwarranted idealization of the past in the face of present difficulties. It is an extravagant expectation on the part of those who owe everything to their God.

The difficulty of grasping the sequence of the events that follow shows that the passage brings together originally separate accounts which have been woven into a single narrative. Nothing is said this time about Moses' crying to Yahweh. Yahweh addresses Moses, announcing that he will rain bread from heaven for them. No reference is made to the murmuring of the people. The purpose of the gift of bread is to prove Israel, to see if the people will obey Yahweh's commands. They are to gather bread each day sufficient for that day's needs; they will find that what they gather on the sixth day will be sufficient for two days.

Yahweh does not tell Moses to repeat these words to the people, and in fact the three speeches to the people that follow do not directly reflect Yahweh's words. In the first (vv. 6-7),

Moses and Aaron tell the people that Yahweh will soon be revealed to them, but do not say how this will take place. They also do not mention that this will constitute a test of Israel's obedience, though we can understand why this point should not be announced in advance. They add what was not explicit in Yahweh's words to Moses: that Yahweh is about to reveal himself because of Israel's murmuring, which was really directed against Yahweh himself and not just Moses and Aaron, who are merely his servants.

The second speech (v. 8) is given by Moses alone. It promises not only bread but also meat. This corresponds more closely to what the people were seeking in their complaint, and the gift of meat and bread is said to result from Yahweh having heard the murmurings. The third speech (vv. 9-10) is delivered by Aaron at Moses' direction, and simply summons the people to assemble for worship, because Yahweh has heard their complaints. They do so, and looking toward the wilderness, see his glory in the cloud.

Then Yahweh addresses Moses again (v. 12). This time he affirms that he has heard Israel's murmurings, and explicitly tells Moses to announce to the people: "At twilight you shall eat flesh, and in the morning you shall be filled with bread; then you shall know that I am the LORD your God." This is especially confusing, since this has already been communicated to the people in the preceding speeches, but at any rate the stage is set for Yahweh to act once again.

He begins by providing meat in the form of quails which come up in the evening and cover the camp. The quails are mentioned only once in this passage, and are apparently given only a single time in order to fulfill the promise and answer Israel's complaint, however unreasonable. The continuing gift is that which appears in the morning. It is not described very clearly: "a fine, flake-like thing" (the meaning of the original is uncertain), "fine as hoarfrost on the ground . . . it was like coriander seed, white, and the taste of it was like wafers made with honey" (vv. 14, 31). Indeed, when the people see it, they ask, "What is it?" (v. 15), and are told by Moses that it is the bread Yahweh has given them to eat.

Moses then uses their question as the occasion for explaining to them what Yahweh has commanded about its use. Each household is to gather enough for each member of the household (this is specified as an "omer" apiece—a little over two liters). As the people proceed to gather it, some take more and some less. But they learn something about the providence of God when they measure what they have gathered, for they find that they each end up with one omer. No one is to save any for the next day. Some try to do so, but find it rotten and full of worms, and incur Moses' wrath for their disobedience. Clearly, God's people are not to be either greedy or miserly, but are to rely on him to provide for each day.

When the people gather their food on the sixth day, they find that, apparently without any special effort on their part, they accumulate twice as much. The leaders come to Moses to tell him about it, and he explains the remainder of what Yahweh has commanded. "Tomorrow is a day of solemn rest, a holy sabbath to the LORD," he says (v. 23). This is an anticipation of the law which Israel is to receive later. They have not been told before about the sabbath or the provisions for observing it. But even now they are to use God's gifts in a way that will honor the sabbath. They are to save enough food from the sixth day to see them through the seventh, and are assured that it will not spoil. They are not to go out on the sabbath, for they will find no food then. As usual, there are some who disobey, going out on the sabbath to gather. These evoke some angry words from Yahweh to Moses, but no punishment. The sabbath commandment is repeated, and the people are given another chance to obey.

In the last part of this section, provision is made to preserve one measure of this otherwise perishable substance (here called "manna"), so that future generations "may see the bread with which I fed you in the wilderness, when I brought you out of the land of Egypt" (v. 32). Moses instructs Aaron to put an omer of manna in a jar. That he then places the jar "before the LORD . . . before the testimony" (vv. 33-34) indicates that this passage is written from the perspective of a later time. These are phrases used of objects associated with the ark, instructions for which are given only later in the Book of Exodus (25:10-22). The same ark which is to contain the tablets of the law, setting forth God's claim on his people, is also to have this reminder of God's gracious provision for his people in the wilderness. This later perspective is also seen in the additional statement that the people ate the manna 40 years, until they entered the promised land and did not need it any more. The contrast is striking: even if their recollection of abundant food in Egypt were not a mere illusion, it would have sustained them only for a life of continuing bondage. But the bread which Yahweh sends from heaven sustains them until they reach a land of their own in freedom. They have to forfeit security, that they may learn to trust Yahweh.

In summary, we note that the chapter suggests a number of different explanations of the significance of the food given in the wilderness. First, it is given as a test for the people. Their complaint could be understood as an attempt to test Yahweh, to see if he can meet their demands. But when he gives them food, he turns the challenge back on them: "that I may prove them, whether they will walk in my law or not" (v. 4). Second, it is given as a revelation of Yahweh's power and glory: "At evening you shall know that it was the LORD that brought you out of the land of Egypt, and in the morning you shall see the glory of the LORD" (vv. 6-7). This revelation contains a hint of judgment on the people for their murmuring; these same phrases are used of Yahweh's deeds against the Egyptians. But it also hints at his gracious identification with Israel: "then you shall know that I am the LORD your God" (v. 12). Finally, it is an expression of his providential care for his people in the hostile environment which was their home for a generation; it is "the bread with which I fed you in the wilderness" (v. 32).

3. Water from the rock (17:1-7).

The people continue on their way; that it is a journey with a destination is indicated by the statement that they moved on "according to the commandment of the LORD" (v. 1). They camp eventually at a place called Rephidim, apparently not far from Sinai. The episode which follows is reminiscent of the earlier one at Marah (15:22-27). There is no water for the people to drink, and again they murmur against Moses.

This time, however, there is an exchange between Moses and the people, before Moses cries to Yahweh. The people find fault with Moses, and demand that he give them water to drink. Moses accuses them of putting Yahweh "to the proof" (v. 2). But they accuse Moses of bringing them up out of Egypt only to kill them with thirst. Their lack of faith is underscored by the fact that they do not even mention Yahweh: "Why did you bring us up out of Egypt?" they ask Moses (v. 3).

After this exchange, Moses cries to Yahweh. His words (v. 4) indicate two things about his state of mind. First, he is exasperated: "What shall I do with this people?" he asks—not *my* people, or even *your* people, but *this* people. Second, he is frightened: "They are almost ready to stone me."

Yahweh's reply is a further demonstration of his patience. "Pass on before the people," he tells Moses (v. 5), thus suggesting that Moses' fear is groundless. These words also indicate the importance of the people being fully aware of what happens next, since their complaints give evidence that they are "putting the LORD to the proof." For this reason, some of the elders are to be taken along as witnesses. Moses continues to act as Yahweh's agent. He is to take in his hand the rod with which he struck the Nile, a rod which in some respects symbolizes the judgment of Yahweh, because of its connection with the plagues. Indeed, the Israelites might well anticipate its use against them now, for by putting Yahweh to the proof they have violated the condition under which he had promised to "put none of the diseases upon you which I put upon the Egyptians" (15:26).

But the rod is used this time for blessing, not for punishment. Yahweh announces that he will precede Moses to the rock at Horeb (it is not clear whether this Horeb is to be understood as "the mountain of God" where Yahweh first appeared to Moses). Moses is to strike the rock, and water will come out of it for the people to drink. This is done, and the elders are witnesses.

Only in the naming of the place is attention called to Israel's sin. Moses calls it Massah and Meribah, words meaning "proof" and "contention." This is said to be "because of the faultfinding of the children of Israel, and because they put the LORD to the proof by saying, 'Is the LORD among us or not?' " (v. 7). They have not said this in so many words, to be sure. But they have failed to trust Yahweh despite all that he has done for them; they have turned against his agent when the going got difficult; and they have made their loyalty to Yahweh conditional on their own comfort and safety. The proper question is not "Is the LORD among us or not?" but "Are we with the LORD or not?" It is not Yahweh who is being tested, but Israel; and Israel has failed the test. Nevertheless, Yahweh has spared them and granted their request.

4. The defeat of Amalek (17:8-16).

As they travel through the wilderness, the people of Israel have faced the dangers presented by the hostility of nature, and have been preserved by Yahweh from both hunger and thirst. Now, for the first time, they face the hostility of the nations, here represented by Amalek. The Amalekites were a desert tribe or people, and several references elsewhere in the Bible describe them as continuing opponents of Israel until well into the period of the monarchy.

When the Amalekites confront the Israelites in the wilderness, arrangements must be made to fight them. Israel has no organized fighting force, so Moses delegates Joshua to choose men for the battle and to lead them. This is the first mention of Joshua, but no information about him is provided because he became so well known as Moses' successor at the end of the wilderness period. Although Moses, by now an old man, does not directly take part in the battle, he promises to stand at the top of the hill with the rod of God, the symbol of God's intervention on Israel's behalf. This plan is not presented as being given by Yahweh, but the end of the episode shows that it is acceptable to him.

Joshua obeys, and Moses goes up the hill, accompanied by Aaron and Hur. The latter, like Joshua, has not been mentioned before but, unlike Joshua, does not have a prominent part to play later on. The importance of Moses' role, even though he is not in the midst of the fighting, is indicated by the effect of the position of his hands. As long as they are raised, Israel takes the lead; when they are lowered, Amalek prevails. So essential to Israel's success is their position that, when Moses grows tired, Aaron and Hur bring a stone for him to sit on and themselves stand on either side to hold up his hands.

No specific explanation of this is given. It is not said, for example, that Moses' hands are raised in prayer, or that they serve as an encouragement to the Israelite troops. But it would not do justice to the text to see Moses as engaged in some kind of magic. Rather, what is being said is that this is no ordinary battle, to be decided by the relative strengths of the opposing forces. Yahweh has a stake in it, just as he has had in Israel's earlier adventures. Working through his chosen agent, he will determine its outcome.

The outcome is as we expect: "Joshua mowed down Amalek and his people with the edge of the sword" (v. 13). When the battle is over, provision is made for its memory to be suitably preserved. Moses is both to write down and also to teach to his successor Joshua that Yahweh "will utterly blot out the remembrance of Amalek from under heaven" (v. 14).

Moses also builds an altar with a name and a dedication intended to perpetuate the same conviction.

This is the first of numerous battles Israel will fight on its way to possession of the promised land. What is distressing to many readers is that Israel is said to enter into these battles at Yahweh's command, and that he fights with them until the enemy is destroyed. But the point of these stories is not that Yahweh is a warlike God, or that he gives his blessing to bloodshed when it is carried out in his name. Still less is it that he allows Israel to use him to sanctify its military adventures. Rather, they express the conviction that the biblical God does not stand aloof from the world in which men and women live, or absent himself from their turbulent activities. He works in and through human beings, sinful human beings, since there is no other kind. He works in and through them at their best and at their worst, as he pursues the fulfillment of his promises and the accomplishment of his universal purpose.

5. A visit from Moses' father-in-law (18:1-27).

Nothing has been said of Moses' family since the end of Exodus 4. Now Jethro, the priest of Midian, Moses' father-in-law, again makes an appearance. He has "heard of all that God had done for Moses and for Israel his people, how the LORD had brought Israel out of Egypt" (v. 1). Because it has been so long since the members of the family have been mentioned, we are given a brief resume. Moses' wife Zipporah is said to have returned to her father's household after being sent away by Moses, presumably when the contest with Pharaoh grew severe. With her were two sons, Gershom (of whom we were told earlier) and Eliezer (who is here mentioned for the first time). The name of each son is interpreted in a way significant for Moses' experience.

Jethro has heard reports of what has happened to Moses and Israel and, now that they have come near to where he lives, he visits them, bringing Zipporah and the boys. It is difficult to know just where this is supposed to be taking place. In chapter 17, Israel was at Rephidim; there they complained about the lack of water and also fought with Amalek. At the beginning of chapter 19, they leave Rephidim and travel to the wilderness of Sinai, where they encamp before "the mountain." But when Jethro arrives, Moses is already encamped at the mountain of God (v. 5). Perhaps we are not intended to take these episodes as coming in chronological order.

At any rate, Moses receives his father-in-law with every sign of honor and affection (nothing is said of his reunion with his wife and sons!), and fills him in on all that Yahweh has done for Israel. Jethro's response is described as fourfold. First, he rejoices "for all the good which the LORD had done to Israel" (v. 9). Second, he blesses Yahweh (v. 10). Third, he confesses, "Now I know that the LORD is greater than all gods" (v. 11). Finally, he "offered a burnt offering and sacrifices to God" (v. 12).

It is not clear from all this how Jethro's relationship to Yahweh is to be understood. Is Yahweh the God whom Jethro has been serving, as priest of Midian, so that he is here pictured as simply coming to a deeper understanding of this God's purpose and activity? Or is Jethro here changing his allegiance and becoming a convert to Yahweh the God of Israel? In any case, his offering and sacrifices to Yahweh are accepted; Aaron and all the elders of Israel come (Moses is already there, of course) "to eat bread with Moses' father-in-law before God" (v. 12). That is, they join Jethro in a fellowship meal which is eaten in front of the altar of sacrifice.

What happens the next day is confirmation that Jethro is accepted as a legitimate representative of Israel's God. He sees Moses judging the people. Nothing has been said about this earlier in the Book of Exodus, but apparently it has become an established procedure. All day long, Moses sits giving judgment and the people stand around him to receive it. Jethro asks Moses about what he sees, and it is clear from his question that he considers it less than satisfactory. Moses replies by describing what takes place: the people come to inquire of God; they bring their disputes to Moses and he decides between the parties, informing them about God's statutes and decisions. Jethro's response is to point out that the arrangement is impractical; it is too much of a burden for Moses to carry, and will wear out both Moses and the people. Jethro then proceeds to give Moses advice about a better way to accomplish the same thing.

His advice is that Moses should continue to do those things which only he has authority to do: "You shall represent the people before God, and bring their cases to God; and you shall teach them the statutes and the decisions, and make them know the way in which they must walk and what they must do" (vv. 19-20). Some functions, however, can be delegated, and this Moses should arrange for by choosing suitable people to be responsible for various segments of the population: "let them judge the people at all times; every great matter they shall bring to you, but any small matter they shall decide themselves; so it will be easier for you, and they will bear the burden with you" (v. 22).

Thus a major change in the life of the community is proposed because a non-Israelite visitor happens to notice that the prevailing practice is inadequate. The new arrangements which he suggests are not said to be based on divine revelation, on any specific set of instructions from Yahweh. Rather, the manner in which they are set forth gives the impression that they derive from Jethro's own common sense and wisdom, perhaps reflecting his experience as priest of Midian. Nevertheless, he emphatically says—to Moses!—"God so commands you" (v. 23). This claim is not disputed, and Moses institutes Jethro's suggestions just as he gave them. The point is that the will of God for the life of his people comes to be known in more than one way. It is not communicated only in moments of explicit divine revelation to the designated leader. It also emerges from the good judgment of those who can offer counsel for the tangible occasions of life in the community.

Part 2

God Makes a Covenant with Israel

Meeting the Deliverer

1. Announcement of the Covenant (19:1-9).

On the first day of the third month after leaving Egypt, Israel arrives at the spot which is to be the setting of all that follows in the Book of Exodus. Only in Numbers 10 do we read of them resuming their journey, after some eleven months at the mountain. That the mountain is the goal of their travels so far is stressed by the careful enumeration of the stages by which they approach it: they *go forth* out of the land of Egypt, *come into* the wilderness of Sinai, *encamp* in the wilderness, and *encamp* before the mountain (vv. 1-2). But only Moses *goes up* to God, a theme which will be developed more fully in the verses that follow.

When Moses goes up, Yahweh calls to him from the mountain, and gives him a message to communicate to the people of Israel. It is brief, but extremely important, because it explains the meaning of what is about to take place. The message begins with a reminder of what Yahweh has done for Israel: "You have seen what I did to the Egyptians, and how I bore you on eagles' wings and brought you to myself." Next is a summary of the challenge with which Israel is about to be confronted: "Now therefore, if you will obey my voice and

keep my covenant . . ." Finally the purpose of all this is set
forth: "you shall be my own possession among all peoples; for
all the earth is mine, and you shall be to me a kingdom of
priests and a holy nation" (vv. 4-6). Thus Yahweh announces
that he is making a covenant—establishing a special relationship—with Israel. This nation is singled out from all other nations; it is unique, a chosen people.

The claim that one group is a chosen people, God's elect,
can be an offensive one, if the implication is that here are some
who are singled out for great privileges from which everyone
else is excluded. It is important to notice how carefully such
arrogance is avoided here. Israel's special relationship to Yahweh is set in the context of his universal sovereignty: "for all
the earth is mine." Yahweh does not say that he is Israel's
possession, to be used for Israel's benefit; Israel is to be "my
own possession," says Yahweh, to be used according to his
will. Nor does Yahweh say that Israel alone is to worship and
serve Yahweh, for its own selfish sake; Israel is to be "a kingdom of priests," whose calling is to minister on behalf of
others. It is to be a "holy nation" in the proper sense of the
word *holy:* consecrated, or set apart, for the service of God.
To be chosen means to be chosen *for others.* The New Testament uses this very passage to set forth the vocation of the
Christian church: "You are a chosen race, a royal priesthood, a
holy nation, God's own people, that you may declare the won-
derful deeds of him who called you out of darkness into his
marvelous light" (1 Peter 2:9).

For Israel to carry out this mission requires commitment:
"if you will obey my voice and keep my covenant." It is important to note, however, that this call for commitment is not
some kind of prerequisite that Israel must meet in order to
qualify for God's choice. God uses his people for the sake of
the world only when they are obedient and reliable. But commitment is possible only in response to God's prior act of
grace. It is the people whom he has already delivered who are
challenged by God and called to his service. The order within

the message Yahweh gives Moses is important: "You have seen what I did . . . if you will obey . . . you shall be . . ." The grace of God is first; then the people can respond.

The importance of the message is given strong emphasis by the fact that, brief as it is, it is provided with a forceful introduction and conclusion. Before the message itself, Moses is told, "Thus you shall say to the house of Jacob, and tell the people of Israel" (v. 3). And after the message, he is instructed, "These are the words which you shall speak to the children of Israel" (v. 6).

Moses follows these instructions, returning and summoning the elders in order to report to them what Yahweh had said. It appears that this is also communicated to all the people, for we read that "all the people answered together and said 'all that the LORD has spoken we will do' " (v. 8). When Moses reports the people's response to Yahweh, Yahweh announces that he will appear in such a way that the people will be made aware of his presence and word. Nevertheless, Moses will play the central role in the revelation to follow. Yahweh appears so that the people may hear when he speaks *to Moses*, and may believe *Moses* when he reports the word of Yahweh.

The importance of Moses' office is a key feature of this section. If the passage is taken as a mere report of a sequence of events, it becomes confusing or even ludicrous. Moses has gone up the mountain in verse 3. He has come down again in verse 7. He has apparently gone back up the mountain in verse 8, because he will be coming down in verse 14. Still another round trip awaits him in verses 20 and 25. None of this trudging back and forth would be necessary, if Yahweh would only speak directly to Israel and observe Israel's response for himself. But that is just the point. Yahweh is quite capable of dealing directly with the people, and does so on many occasions. But he has chosen to work through Moses, not only in the deliverance from Egyptian bondage, but also in the establishment of the covenant. The way the story is told makes that clear.

2. Preparations for the meeting with Yahweh (19:10-25).

Moses is now told that Yahweh will appear before Israel on Mount Sinai on the third day. Although the wilderness of Sinai has been mentioned before, this is the first time the mountain itself is clearly designated with that name (16:1 is ambiguous in this regard). It is apparently identified with Horeb, the name of the mountain of God where Yahweh first appeared to Moses in the burning bush.

The entire narrative of the Book of Exodus makes it clear that Yahweh is not a mere territorial God, whose sovereignty is restricted to a particular patch of land where he holds sway. Yahweh has demonstrated that he is in control of the forces of nature and the inhabitants of that great world-power Egypt, and has just asserted that "all the earth is mine" (v. 5). Nevertheless, there is some special association between this God and this place. He had told Moses, at the burning bush, that he was standing on holy ground. Now the people are to be warned that the mountain shares to some degree in the holiness of Yahweh himself, so they may approach only after careful preparation, and then only at the time and up to the point permitted. Moses is to mark out a boundary around the mountain, beyond which the people are not to go until the trumpet gives the signal that they may approach.

In the meantime, the "holy nation" (v. 6) is to be "made holy" by Moses (the word given in our translation as "consecrate" in vv. 10 and 14 is from the same root as the word translated "holy" in v. 6). What that involves is suggested by the two items mentioned in the passage: the people are to wash their garments and abstain from sexual relations, thus marking off the coming occasion as a special one. Moses then goes to the people and carries out the instructions.

These preparations, and the meeting with Yahweh which they anticipate, are presented in terms alien to our usual way of thinking. But the passage serves to emphasize some points which are essential to the biblical understanding of Yahweh and his relation to humanity. Yahweh is God, not a human being. He is not approached casually, on terms of equality, but comes to men and women on his initiative. The experience of his presence requires preparation and awakens awe. Heaven touches earth where God meets his people. Such moments cannot simply be taken in stride.

Despite all of the solemnity, however, Yahweh's coming to his people is not presented as an end in itself, as though the experience of divine presence were the essence of the relationship between Yahweh and Israel. As he says to Moses, "Lo, I am coming to you . . . that the people may hear" (v. 9). The appearance is for the sake of the instruction which is to follow.

The third day brings the promised thick cloud, along with supplementary thunder and lightning, and also the trumpet blast signalling that the people may approach the mountain. As the people draw closer, the accompanying effects become more and more awesome. Finally, Moses speaks and Yahweh answers him in thunder, thus fulfilling the promise of v. 9 and confirming Moses' role.

At this point, we expect to be told what God says to Moses. But before that is done, we are presented with one further episode. Moses is again summoned to the top of the mountain, where he is told to go right back down again and warn the people not to come too close to the divine presence on the mountain. He is also told to make sure that the priests consecrate themselves properly (no priests have yet been appointed, so far as the narrative has told us, but the point is that even those who minister constantly in the presence of the holy— perhaps *especially* those who do so!—are not to let familiarity breed contempt).

For the first time since the aftermath of the initial, unsuccessful interview with Pharaoh, Moses raises a protest to Yahweh. Is this a touch of humor on the part of the biblical author, who wants us to see the amusing side of Moses' being made to run up and down the mountain on what might seem to be unnecessary errands? "The people cannot come up to Mount Sinai," Moses reminds Yahweh, "for thou thyself didst charge us, saying, 'Set bounds about the mountain, and conse-crate it' " (v. 23). But Moses has missed the point. This episode reemphasizes the holiness of Yahweh, and in the process gives further testimony to the centrality of Moses' role. So Yahweh simply repeats his command—"Go down"—and adds that when Moses comes back he should bring Aaron with him. Moses obeys without further protest.

God's Word for His People

1. Introduction (20:1-2).

This passage begins the words of Yahweh from the mountain. We are not told specifically to whom these words are spoken; the text reads simply "And God spoke all these words." But the context suggests that they were addressed to all the people of Israel. For in the preceding section, as we have seen, the people prepare carefully and then draw near (but not *too* near) the mountain. This is done in anticipation of the fulfillment of the divine word to Moses: "Lo, I am coming to you in a thick cloud, that the people may hear when I speak with you, and may also believe you for ever" (19:9). And in the section that follows these words, the people tremble with fear and ask Moses to speak to them, so that they do not have to hear God's voice directly.

If these words of God, then, are spoken to all the people of Israel, they are set apart from the words of God which follow and which are communicated through Moses. We shall see that there are some other indications as well that such a distinction is intended. But already our attention is focused on these verses as in some way central to Yahweh's revelation at the mountain.

What we have before us is, of course, the best-known part of the entire Book of Exodus. It has been memorized and recited by countless generations as the "Ten Commandments" or the "Decalogue." The commandments are not individually numbered anywhere in the Bible (though it is elsewhere said that there are ten of them; see 34:28, and also Deut. 4:13 and 10:4). So it has come about that, in the various groups that use this passage, different numbering systems are used. This is a little confusing, but it is an external matter. Jew and Christian, Catholic and Protestant and Orthodox are all in agreement as to the content of the Decalogue.

God's opening words are not, strictly speaking, a commandment at all, but a statement or affirmation. This serves as a reminder that the Bible itself does not refer to the passage as "commandments" but as "words." Thus in the Jewish tradition this opening statement is called the "first word," and that is an appropriate designation, however one may number the commandments that follow.

The first word affirms God's gracious act of deliverance; "I am the LORD your God, who brought you out of the land of Egypt, out of the house of bondage." This underlines a point made earlier (in connection with 19:4-6): that Yahweh first acts *for* his people before he demands anything *from* them. Indeed, it is only after he has delivered them from bondage in the land of Egypt that they are free to serve him. This explains why, after Egypt is here identified by name, it is further described as "the house of bondage." In the original, the same term underlies the word "bondage" as the word "service." The people who have been delivered from oppressive and life-destroying service to Pharaoh have now come, as promised, to "serve God upon this mountain" (3:12). The very different character of that service is about to be defined. What follows is not a set of obligations marking a return to slavery. It is, on the contrary, a charter of freedom.

2. The commandments (20:3-17).

"You shall have no other gods before me," the commandments begin (v. 3). Before asking about the specific meaning of the verse, we may note some features which will also appear in some or all of the commandments that follow. First of all, it is addressed to Israel: "You. . . ." It is not some universal law, binding on all human beings by virtue of their humanity. Yahweh is setting forth his Word for the people who have been delivered by his grace. Indeed, it is even more pointed than that. For the command is in the singular, not the plural. That is why older translations had "Thou," although our word "you" now does duty as both singular and plural. The point is that Yahweh is not addressing himself to Israel in general, but to every individual Israelite. It is not enough that the community in general should observe these commandments; every member of the community, without exception, is called to obedience.

Second, this commandment (and most of those that follow) is negative in form; it is a prohibition. That does not mean that it represents a restrictive code of behavior. Negative commands allow greater freedom than positive ones, because they assume that what is not forbidden is permitted. By their largely negative form, the Ten Commandments define the outer limits of the covenant—those things which set the transgressor outside the relationship between Yahweh and his people.

Third, this commandment is very brief. It does not define or qualify what it says, or allow for exceptions, or specify rewards for those who obey it or punishment for those who do not. This was probably originally the case with all of these commandments, although some of them (as we shall see) have been expanded into a somewhat fuller form. This brevity and generality of the commandments points us to an understanding of the function of the Decalogue. It is not a law code, which would apply the Word of God to the specific conditions of life in the community and give instructions for the administration of justice. Other collections of laws, which may have served such functions, are present in the Bible, and we shall have opportunity later on to consider one example.

The Decalogue, however, states the Word of God in terms sufficiently broad to rise above many of the particulars of time and place. Of course, even the Ten Commandments are not timeless and abstract; they reflect something of their setting in the ancient world. But they seem to have been formulated in such a way as to minimize such factors, and thus to provide a permanent point of reference in working out a way of life for God's people appropriate to the changing circumstances in which they will live.

Other gods

We turn now to the content of the first commandment. "You shall have no other gods before me" means, in effect, that Yahweh is to have exclusive claim on Israel's worship and service. It does not deny that there are other gods. Israel was surrounded by other gods and their claims on their worshipers. Israel would of course come to recognize that these were not "real" gods, that they did not actually exist as deities. But it was true, and remains true, that even gods that are not real can absorb the attention and energies of those who are devoted to them. The people of Yahweh are forbidden to have such other gods.

Graven images

"You shall not make for yourself a graven image," the passage continues (v. 4). Since other gods have already been prohibited in the previous verse, this must be a prohibition of any image of *Yahweh*. Graven images are those carved from wood or stone. In order to avoid the possible misunderstanding that other representations are permissible, an additional phrase forbids "any likeness" of anything in the entire universe. Although the Old Testament is consistent in its opposition to visual representations of Yahweh, it does not explain the reasons for the opposition, and we are left to speculate. To depict Yahweh in the form of some natural object would be to reduce the Creator to the level of a creature. To depict him even in some abstract image would be to limit him to a particular place and run the risk of thinking that he is at our disposal and subject to our manipulation. There is no way to escape such dangers altogether, if we are to think or speak of God at all. But to make *physical* representations of God is, from the point of view of this commandment, to take a needless risk.

The words that follow (vv. 5-6) are best understood as providing a conclusion for both of the preceding prohibitions, since they not only forbid bowing down to or serving images, but also refer to Yahweh's exclusive claim on Israel's loyalty. The phrase "for I the LORD your God am a jealous God" is somewhat disturbing to modern ears, in view of our largely pejorative use of the term "jealousy." But it is meant to evoke the metaphor of Yahweh as Israel's spouse (for marriage is also a kind of covenant), who expects his beloved to be completely faithful to him, as he is to her.

More disturbing is the warning that follows: that Yahweh is a God "visiting the iniquity of the fathers upon the children to the third and the fourth generation of those who hate me." There is no way to remove all offense from these words, for they speak, after all, of the judgment of God. It is helpful to remember, however, that they are addressed to members of a community with which Yahweh is making a covenant. They do not speak of individual retribution. As we noted earlier, each individual is summoned to obey—to make his or her contribution to the relationship between Yahweh and Israel. But the fruits of the covenant are harvested by the whole community. A typical Israelite household consisted of three or four generations living together in an "extended family." What is being said is that disobedience to the will of God has its destructive consequences for a wider circle, including those most dear to the offender. It is also helpful to remember that judgment is balanced (and, in fact, greatly outweighed) by mercy. If the effects of Yahweh's wrath are felt by three or four generations, his steadfast love extends to thousands of generations—that is, for ever.

Taking the name in vain

The next commandment reads, "You shall not take the name of the LORD your God in vain" (v. 7). Again, the brevity of the verse seems designed to allow for the widest possible application. At its heart is the holiness of the divine name. When we considered the revelation of the name to Moses at the burning bush, we saw how intimately it was related to the character of this God, who makes his name known to Israel as a mark of gracious commitment to them as his people, but in such a way as not to compromise his sovereign freedom. "This is my name for ever," he said then, "and thus I am to be remembered to all generations" (3:15).

But to know Yahweh's name is not a license to utilize it for any selfish or trivial purpose. At various times and in various places, God's name has been incorporated in magical incantations, formulas of cursing and blessing, the taking of oaths, social and political and military ceremonies, and the like—often without regard for his will and purposes. To take his name "in vain" is quite different from invoking it in order to "remember" him. To speak it, whether deliberately or carelessly, in order to secure the sanction of religion for one's own purpose is to attempt to use God and his power for our own ends. This would be similar to the making of an image or likeness of him, though in a more subtle way. Perhaps because it is so subtle, and has to do more with inner motivation than with outward acts as such, this commandment is reinforced with an added warning: "for the LORD will not hold him guiltless who takes his name in vain."

Sabbath

As the story has developed in the Book of Exodus, the people have already been introduced to the sabbath (16:22-30). So the next commandment does not present it as something new and unheard of, but instructs the people to "Remember the sabbath day, to keep it holy" (v. 8). This is the first of only two positive commands (v. 12 is the other). Without compromising the basically negative character of the Decalogue (the significance of which was discussed earlier), the presence of these positive commands suggests an additional dimension. In addition to those things which are excluded from the life of the covenant community, there are other things which are essential to it and give it a distinctive character.

The sabbath is to be kept holy—that is, set apart or consecrated. This presupposes that no work is to be done on this day. The Hebrew term is derived from a word which means "rest, cease from work." The story of the manna describes how receiving a double portion on the previous day made it unnecessary to gather on the sabbath. The prohibition of work on the sabbath is made explicit in the verses (9-11) which follow the commandment itself, which even list seven individuals or groups on whom it is binding: Israelite householder, son, daughter, manservant, maidservant, cattle, and sojourner.

Rest from work is a presupposition for keeping the day holy, but is not sufficient in itself. The additional component is suggested by the last part of the addition to the commandment (v. 11). There a reason is given for keeping the sabbath: "for in six days the LORD made heaven and earth, the sea, and all that is in them, and rested the seventh day; therefore the LORD blessed the sabbath day and hallowed it." Six days a week, God's people may work to subdue the earth (Gen. 1:28), thus joining God in his creative activity. But on the seventh day, like God himself, they are to cease from work and contemplate the goodness of creation.

It should be noted, in connection with the matter of keeping the sabbath, that there is a variation on this commandment elsewhere in the Bible. The Ten Commandments also appear in Deuteronomy 5:6-21. There the commandments themselves are virtually identical to the Exodus version. The reason given for keeping the sabbath, however, is as follows: "You shall remember that you were a servant in the land of Egypt, and the LORD your God brought you out thence with a mighty hand and an outstretched arm; therefore the LORD your God commanded you to keep the sabbath day" (Deut. 5:15). It is in order to remember their deliverance from slavery that the people of Israel are to keep the sabbath. Apparently the original commandment is the brief imperative of v. 8, which could then be expanded in more than one way, depending on the emphasis appropriate to a particular occasion.

Parents

The familiar distinction between the "two tables" of the law, the former comprising duties toward God, and the latter, duties toward fellowhumans, should not be pressed too far. They are all duties toward God, in the sense that they are all commanded by God as the appropriate way of life for his covenant people. And they are all duties toward fellow humans, in the sense that they are inseparable components of a community way of life which will provide maximum well-being for all of its members.

That being said, however, it can be acknowledged that there is a change of focus as one proceeds from the first to the last commandments. In the shift of focus from God to fellow humans, the next commandment marks the transition. "Honor your father and your mother," it reads (v. 12). The status of parents is not defined, but the position of the commandment speaks for itself. Furthermore, the promise which is attached leads to some reflections on the subject: "that your days may be long in the land which the LORD your God gives you." God and parents are associated here as the ones to whom a person owes both life itself and the support of life.

That which is to be given to father and mother is purposely left quite broad in scope. The term "honor" is sufficient to cover the changing obligations that are appropriate as off-spring grow from childhood to adulthood, and as parents pass from full vigor to the increasing dependency of age. In addition, we should not take "father and mother" in isolation from the whole extended family, that network of near and distant relations with whom one has ties of gratitude and obligation.

Murder, adultery, theft

The next three commandments are "You shall not kill, you shall not commit adultery, you shall not steal" (vv. 13-15). They resemble each other in their unadorned straightforwardness. The paradoxical result of this stark simplicity is that these commandments are easier to understand (at least in regard to their basic meaning) than some of the others, but also lead to more pressing questions. Clearly they place under divine protection certain matters crucial to the well-being of society—life itself, the marriage bond, the possessions which persons may justly call their own. But it is not so clear exactly what they are intended to prohibit.

So we naturally are led to raise questions. "You shall not kill." Of course this forbids cold-blooded deliberate murder. But what about self-defense, defense of others, participation in war, capital punishment, abortion, or "mercy-killing"? "You shall not commit adultery." Of course this forbids sexual relations between two persons, each of whom is married to someone else. But what about sexual relations between unmarried persons, remarriage after divorce, or homosexual relations? "You shall not steal." Of course this forbids armed robbery or breaking and entering. But what about concealment of flaws in merchandise, misrepresentation in advertising, or usury? Furthermore, in regard to all three of these commandments, what is to be the penalty for transgression? Are there ever extenuating circumstances which would justify a lighter penalty, or none at all?

The answers to such questions are not obvious. Nevertheless, society must have answers, if it is to achieve order and preserve it in the circumstances of its own time and place. It is the function of codes of law to set forth the answers in the light of given situations. We have seen, however, that the function of the Ten Commandments is not to be a law code, but to announce the terms of the covenant. By itself, it cannot answer these questions, though it provides the basis on which the people of God will answer them.

False witness

The commandment "You shall not bear false witness against your neighbor" (v. 16) uses the language of the law court. Not bearing false witness means not making false accusations or statements that might lead to an unjust verdict. But what is added to the meaning by the phrase "against your neighbor"? Conceivably, this might be a way of limiting the scope of the commandment, as if to say, "You shall not bear false witness against your neighbor—but you may do so against others." It is true that there are passages in the Old Testament in which the word for "neighbor" is used to mean "fellow Israelite," in contrast to others. But that is not always the case (in 11:2, for example, the Egyptians are called "neighbors" of the Israelites). Furthermore, in the Decalogue itself, the sabbath is also to be a day of rest for "the sojourner who is within your gates" (v. 10); presumably the commandment against false witness will not be more restrictive. To interpret it in such a way as to exclude non-Israelites from its protection would be inconsistent with the dictum, "There shall be one law for the native and for the stranger who sojourns among you" (12:49).

The phrase "against your neighbor" does not, therefore, limit the scope of the commandment. Rather, it serves to explain and emphasize the importance of a prohibition which might otherwise be brushed aside as less vital than the previous three. Murder, adultery, and theft are concrete, physical acts which quite directly injure one's neighbor. False witness is, or can be, more indirect and subtle. But the fact that it is a matter of word and not deed does not make it any less damaging. It is "against your neighbor."

Coveting

Not only is it forbidden to harm the neighbor by deed or word; it is also forbidden to do so by thought. That is a significant aspect of the next commandment, "You shall not covet your neighbor's house" (v. 17). The word here translated "house" means more than just real estate; it means "household," and includes the items identified in the list that follows: "You shall not covet your neighbor's wife, or his manservant, or his maidservant, or his ox, or his ass, or anything that is your neighbor's." If coveting were only the outward activity by which one seeks to gain possession of that which belongs to one's neighbor, it would already be sufficiently covered by other commandments: "You shall not commit adultery, you shall not steal." But coveting includes the inner motivation that leads to the outward act. The inclusion of a commandment which prohibits the very desires that result in evil words and deeds reveals the comprehensive nature of the covenant Yahweh is making with Israel.

3. Israel's reaction (20:18-21).

This passage follows the Ten Commandments which, as we noted earlier, are to be understood as spoken by God in the hearing of all the people. It describes not just what happens after God finishes speaking, but the people's reaction throughout his entire appearance. Thus the passage begins by recalling the awesome signs of the divine presence, already mentioned in Exodus 19: "the thunderings and the lightnings and the sound of the trumpet and the mountain smoking" (20:18).

Also, it follows through on a key theme of Exodus 19: the importance of Moses' office.

The people respond to God's presence and words with fear and trembling. Instead of presuming to push closer than permitted (as 19:21 might lead us to expect), they stand afar off. Furthermore, they ask Moses to speak to them, presumably on God's behalf, and promise to listen to him; "but let not God speak to us, lest we die" (v. 19). In Exodus 19, Yahweh acted to demonstrate that Moses is his spokesman, "that the people may hear when I speak with you, and may also believe you for ever" (19:9). Now the people confirm by their own words their acceptance of Moses in this role.

Moses is concerned, however, that the people not have the wrong motive for desiring such a spokesman. They are afraid, but Moses tells them "Do not fear" (v. 20). They seem to think that God intends to destroy them, but Moses reassures them. "God has come to prove you," he says—to test, in other words, whether they were sincere when they promised, "All that the LORD has spoken we will do" (19:8). Furthermore, God has come "that the fear of him may be before your eyes, that you may not sin." That seems odd, since Moses has just told them not to fear. But there is a distinction between the fear that keeps them standing afar off and the fear that keeps them from sin. In the Bible, the fear of God in the proper sense is obedience to God. Having made this point, Moses does as the people request and approaches the divine presence.

God's Word Applied to the World of the Day

1. Introduction (20:22).

This section begins with the words, "And the LORD said to Moses, 'Thus you shall say to the people of Israel. . . .'" The implication is that Yahweh now considers as settled the role of Moses as spokesman. Yahweh established the arrangement, and the people confirmed it. From now on, Yahweh will speak to Moses, and Moses will speak to the people. So that the people will accept the word that comes through Moses, he is to begin with this reminder from Yahweh: "You have seen for yourselves that I have talked with you from heaven."

This verse provides the heading for all that follows, through the end of Exodus 23. That Exodus 24 begins a new section can be seen from the fact that it has its own heading: "And he said to Moses . . ." (24:1).

2. The ordinances (20:23—23:19).

The material we now have before us is known as "The Book of the Covenant," because of the reference in 24:7. It is sometimes also known as "The Covenant Code." This suggests that it is a law code. But this is not altogether accurate, even though we can see at a glance that it contains legal material. We shall discover, however, that there is more than one kind of law here, and that the passage is not comprehensive and well-organized in the manner of a modern law code. The meaning and purpose of the Book of the Covenant will emerge more clearly as we examine its contents.

The next verse (20:23) is a link between what comes before and what comes after. Like the preceding verse, it addresses the people of Israel in the plural ("you"); the community has just witnessed Yahweh speaking from heaven, and now is reminded that this God is not to be depicted in an idol nor made to share his place with idols: "You shall not make gods of silver to be with me, nor shall you make for yourselves gods of gold." This leads into the following verses which, although they use the first person singular ("thou," in older English versions) also have to do with proper worship.

Altars (20:24-26)

Specifically, they have to do with the construction of altars. Sacrificial altars are to be made of earth, and only in those places designated by Yahweh as suitable for worshiping him. If stone altars are constructed, only unhewn stones (rather than dressed ones) are to be used. Altars are not to be approached by steps. No reasons are given for these regulations (unless the concluding phrase of 20:26 is a partial explanation for prohibiting steps). But it is probable that they are intended to prevent Israel from taking over pagan altars from the earlier inhabitants of the land to which they are going. The danger is, of course, that beliefs and practices will be carried over which are incompatible with the worship of Yahweh.

It is instructive to compare these laws with the laws in the Decalogue, especially 20:3-4 to which they are most closely related. There is a similarity in form: brief statements without explanation, qualification, or penalty. The difference lies in the greater *particularity* of this passage—that is, it gives more specific instructions for applying the Word of God in a concrete historical situation. It answers the question of how Israel is to conduct itself in a world in which gold and silver idols and pagan altars abound. The more general character of the Ten Commandments is apparent.

Slaves (21:1-11)

The opening verse of Exodus 21 does not constitute a new heading, such as we have in 20:22 and 24:2, but designates what follows as "ordinances." This term may originally have been used for the type of laws that immediately follow in 21:1—22:17; as we shall see, they are different in form from the others in the Book of the Covenant. But in its present context it distinguishes the entire Book of the Covenant from the Decalogue (the ten "words," 20:1). That is the usage, at any rate, at the beginning of the next section, where we read that "Moses came and told the people all the words of the LORD and all the ordinances" (24:3).

The form of the laws which follow can be readily seen to be different from the unconditional imperatives of the Ten Commandments or the laws about altars. Each of them describes a certain situation, beginning with the word "When," and states the basic law that governs it. Special conditions which may arise are then described, beginning with the word "If," and the way in which they modify the law follows. This form is ideally suited for application to specified particular conditions.

It is important to be clear about the function of these laws concerning slavery. They do not establish the institution of slavery, or, indeed, make any general pronouncement about it. They are directed to a society in which slavery was a fact of life, and are intended to regulate it. In Israel there were people who were slaves because their impoverished parents had been compelled to sell them into slavery, or because they had been forced into it by their own poverty, or because they had been sentenced to it in punishment for theft. The first of these two laws (vv. 2-6) provides that no one is to be trapped in permanent bondage; after six years a slave is to go free, without the need to buy that freedom. The special conditions have to do with married slaves and slaves who wish to remain in the service of their master. The second law (vv. 7-11) provides that a woman who is a slave and has become a concubine to her master or his son cannot simply be sent away, but is entitled to special status and treatment. It goes without saying that a slave-holding society is not an ideal one. But these laws serve to moderate the dehumanizing effects of the institution.

Capital offenses (21:12-17)

Most of the laws in 21:1—22:17 are of the type which we have just seen in the preceding passage. These verses concerning capital offenses constitute the only exception. They follow the form "Whoever does so-and-so shall be put to death." The offenses dealt with are murder, striking father or mother, kidnapping, and cursing (more accurately, dishonoring) father or mother. The only qualification is introduced in the case of the first of these laws. There it is recognized that one person may cause the death of another by accident (the phrase "God let him fall into his hand" [v. 13] means roughly what we mean when we call an accident "an act of God"). In a society in which the task of executing a murderer fell to the dead person's family, this law provides a sanctuary for an accused who wishes to plead that it was an accident. But the sanctuary, at a place where Yahweh is worshiped, is not intended for those who kill deliberately.

These laws may seem to us to be excessively severe, living as we do in a time when the death penalty has been abolished in many places. We should note, however, that the ones which seem to us most excessive—namely, those which have to do with striking or cursing parents—do not refer to the actions of little children who occasionally throw temper tantrums. They are concerned with violent disruptions in the life of a society largely organized around extended families and the authority of the heads of these families. It is the stability of this family structure that is being protected here.

In any case, we need to understand all of these commandments in the context of a world in which capital punishment was enacted for a wide variety of offenses, especially when committed by the common people. Here only a few acts, judged to be utterly destructive of the life of the covenant community, have this penalty attached. All of them deal with matters also dealt with in the Decalogue; violators have transgressed against the outer limits of the covenant and placed themselves outside the covenant community. The overall effect is a moderation of practices prevailing in the ancient world.

Bodily injury (21:18-32)

This passage continues the type of laws with which the chapter began. Although the form is the same, the subject here is bodily injury, both of free persons and of slaves. Clearly these few laws are not intended to provide a complete and systematic treatment of this whole aspect of life, but only to give a few examples to serve as a guide.

Injuries that occur during fights are dealt with in vv. 18-19 and 22-25. When two persons fight and one is injured, the other is to provide compensation for loss of time and for medical expenses. When two persons fight and a bystander is injured (the rather specialized example given here is of a woman who suffers a miscarriage), there is also to be compensation. If, however, the injury is permanent, a further penalty follows for the one who inflicted it: "If any harm follows, then you shall give life for life, eye for eye, tooth for tooth, hand for hand, foot for foot, burn for burn, wound for wound, stripe for stripe" (vv. 23-25).

The way in which the principle is formulated makes it clear that it is intended for much wider application than to the case of a pregnant woman hurt in a brawl. Taken without regard for context, it seems primitive and brutal; and, indeed, a rigid application in all circumstances could not be justified. But it represents a step forward in a world in which the rich and privileged could inflict injury on those of lower social status and escape punishment simply by the payment of a fine. The principle stated here provides equality before the law and protection for those most in need of it.

Injuries to slaves are the subject of vv. 20-21 and 26-27. Once it is recognized that slavery is intrinsically evil, laws intended to regulate it can have only relative moral value. And once slavery is abolished, such laws can have only historical interest. Here it is sufficient to note that in Israel, unlike some other ancient societies, a slave-owner who caused the death of a slave was punished and a slave-owner who caused permanent injury (even such a comparatively minor one as loss of a tooth) was compelled to let the injured slave go free.

The remaining laws in this passage deal with fatal injuries caused by oxen. Even more than the laws already considered, they testify to the way in which the Book of the Covenant reflects a society very different from our own. The main stipulation is that an ox which gores a person to death is to be killed. The responsibility of the owner of the ox hinges on whether or not negligence was involved. An interesting point is that, while the formal penalty for a negligent owner is death, the survivors of the person killed may accept compensation instead. One suspects that they would usually prefer that alternative.

Property damage (21:33—22:17)

The kinds of property damage dealt with in these verses, and the dependence of the laws on the circumstances of life in ancient Israel, make it unnecessary for our purposes to consider them in detail. It will be sufficient to note the range of damages dealt with, along with certain features of broader significance.

The first verses (21:33-36) deal with responsibility for negligence leading to the death of livestock belonging to another. Then follows (22:1,4) the setting of penalties for stealing of livestock; here it is worth noting that the penalties involve restitution and additional compensation, even to the extent of selling the thief into slavery if he cannot otherwise pay, but the death penalty is not invoked.

We next note (22:2-3) the case of the thief found breaking and entering. Because property is always of less value than life, the concern here is with the violence that may accompany discovery of the thief. There is a balance of concern for the life of the householder and the life of the thief. If the thief is discovered at night and killed, no blame attaches to the householder, since the death is considered a necessary act of self-defense. But if the thief is discovered in the daylight, the assumption is that the householder's life is not in danger, and the killing of the thief carries blame.

The following verses (22:5-6) concern damage to others' fields by domestic animals or fire. After this come provisions (22:7-15) governing the responsibilities of those who have been entrusted with the care of goods or animals belonging to others, or who have borrowed such goods or services.

Finally, there are two verses (22:16-17) that deal with the seduction of an unbetrothed virgin. The fact that this subject appears at the end of the passage dealing with property damage seems to place this offense in the category of economics—as does the reference to the "marriage present" or bride price (otherwise seldom mentioned in the Old Testament). But it is clear that it is not *merely* a sin against property. The man who seduces an unbetrothed virgin must give the marriage present for her *and* marry her. In other words, he must take full responsibility for the consequences of his act. Only if the father considers the marriage unsuitable (in ancient Israel, as in many societies, the father acted on behalf of his daughter) is the man released from the obligation to marry the woman, although he still must pay an equivalent sum.

Miscellaneous (22:18-31)

The rest of the Book of the Covenant consists of laws similar in form to those which we considered in the passages on altars and capital offenses. First (vv. 18-20) are three laws which closely resemble those in 21:12-17, not only in form but also in content, since they also specify capital offenses. The offenses appear unrelated to each other, but bestiality was often associated with magical practices in the ancient world, and magic with idolatry. So they all may be considered to deal with the same subject as the opening verses of the Decalogue.

Next (vv. 21-27) come laws intended to protect those who are weak and vulnerable: strangers, widows and orphans, and the poor. The Israelites are not to wrong a stranger, for they were strangers in Egypt. They are not to afflict widows or orphans, for Yahweh will hear and avenge them. And they are to lend money to the poor without interest and without taking in pledge what the poor need for survival, for the poor are also part of "my people" and will be heard by Yahweh.

The last of the laws in this passage (vv. 28-31) are loosely connected with the idea of honoring God. It is forbidden to revile God or the ruler who derives his authority from God. There is to be no delay in offering the firstfruits of the vineyard or the firstborn of man and beast. As people consecrated to God, they are not to eat meat from an animal not properly slaughtered. Once again we see the incomplete and illustrative character of this collection of laws.

Justice (23:1-9)

These laws having to do with justice begin and end with instructions about court procedure. The opening verses (vv. 1-3) first warn against uttering a false report (presumably on one's own initiative), next against being involved in a partnership in which a wicked person prevails on one to give false testimony, and then against being swayed by the prevailing opinion to contribute to a miscarriage of justice. Finally, and rather subtly, they warn against a kind of misapplied sympathy that would favor the suit brought by a poor person, regardless of where justice lies. These warnings are directed toward witnesses.

The closing verses (vv. 6-9), on the other hand, are directed toward judges. They warn against favoring the rich, accepting false charges, convicting the innocent, acquitting the wicked, accepting bribes, and oppressing strangers.

Between these two blocks of material are two verses (vv. 4-5) which serve as a reminder that justice is not limited to the formal setting of a court of law. They also point out that justice involves more than refraining from unjust actions; it requires active doing of good, even to one who may not be well-disposed toward oneself. The example chosen to make this point reflects the world of biblical times, as we might expect; but it is vivid enough to merit quoting here: "If you meet your enemy's ox or his ass going astray, you shall bring it back to him. If you see the ass of one who hates you lying under its burden, you shall refrain from leaving him with it, you shall help him to lift it up."

Sacred seasons (23:10-19)

The last of the laws in the Book of the Covenant have to do with observances related to the calendar. Agricultural land, including vineyards, is to be used for six years and then allowed to "rest" for a year. Whatever it produces spontaneously in that seventh year is not to be gathered by the farmer, but left for the poor and the wild beasts. The weekly sabbath is to be kept, for the benefit of animals, servants, and resident aliens. Three agricultural festivals are to be kept, at which time "shall all your males appear before the Lord GOD" (vs. 17). Some instructions regarding offerings bring this passage to an end.

It is significant that the opening and closing laws in the

Book of the Covenant concern "cultic" matters, that is, matters of formal religious observance. In contrast, the intervening laws deal with the affairs of everyday life, most of them without any mention of Yahweh or his covenant with Israel. These latter laws are what we might call "secular" in content—if it were not for the fact that the context makes a "sacred/secular" distinction irrelevant. Israel's life is a unity. All of it comes under the sovereignty of Yahweh. Whether one is building an altar, or compensating a neighbor for damage to crops by one's stray livestock, or making a loan to a person in need, one does so before God. Everything in the life of this community and all its members is to testify to the covenant—the relationship between this God and the people whom he has chosen, delivered, and called.

3. Conclusion (23:20-33).

Although these verses bring the Book of the Covenant to an end, they are not what we might expect by way of a conclusion. We find here no reference to the laws which comprise the preceding chapters. Rather, we find a look forward to Israel in the promised land, which is presented as the gift of Yahweh to his people, but which they will occupy in security and prosperity only if they are faithful to Yahweh and his Word.

There is a connection between this passage and what immediately precedes it. The "sacred seasons" set forth in 23:10-19 are to be observed in the land, and this passage gives promises and warnings relating to the land. But it is more to the point to note the way in which the entire presentation of the law thus far—both Decalogue and Book of the Covenant, both "words" and "ordinances"—is enclosed by references to land. The Decalogue begins with a reminder of deliverance from one land: "I am the LORD your God, who brought you out of the land of Egypt" (20:2). The Book of the Covenant ends with a promise to bring his people up to another land: "to bring you to the place which I have prepared" (23:20). Thus, the grace of God, expressed in salvation and blessing, is the context for the giving of the law. The word of Yahweh at the burning bush (3:7-8) is confirmed by the promised sign: "You shall serve God upon this mountain" (3:12).

The Covenant
Confirmed – and Broken

1. Instructions to Moses (24:1-2).

Yahweh has been speaking to Moses, so that the opening phrase of this section ("And he said to Moses") appears to be unnecessary. But the preceding chapters (beginning with 20:22) consist of matters which Moses is to communicate to the people, while those that follow are addressed to Moses personally.

The instructions to Moses involve some careful distinctions based on closeness of approach to Yahweh. The people must stay where they are (judging by their earlier reaction, they are probably content to do so). Moses is to bring Aaron, his two sons, and seventy elders, and "come up" (presumably, further up the mountain). Only Moses, however, is to "come near." These instructions emphasize the holiness of Yahweh and the special status of those who represent the people before him. More important, they reiterate Moses' unique office as that was presented in Exodus 19 and 20:18-21.

2. The covenant-making ceremony (24:3-8).

Before following the instructions, Moses communicates to the people what he has received from Yahweh. He tells them "all the words of the LORD and all the ordinances" (v. 3); that is, the Ten Commandments and the Book of the Covenant.

He also writes these down, and then reads them in the hearing of the people. Although slightly different terminology is used each time, we are probably not to understand distinctions among what he told, what he wrote, and what he read out. The point is, rather, to emphasize that the people are fully and precisely informed about the obligations of the covenant into which they are entering.

This is a suitable point at which to discuss more directly a matter that has been alluded to several times, and that is the relationship between the Decalogue and the other laws which are here presented to Israel. That they are not to be seen as all of the same sort is already implied in the different terms employed: "words" for one, "ordinances" for the other. Further evidence for a distinction is to be seen in the fact that the Ten Commandments are described as spoken by Yahweh in the hearing of all the people, while the people first hear the other laws through Moses. Although not completely distinct in the forms of the laws they contain, the Ten Commandments are, for the most part, brief, unconditional, and include no penalties, while the Book of the Covenant contains a high proportion of laws which set forth particular conditions and lay down penalties for violation. In content, the Decalogue is much more general and much less tied to the social and cultural circumstances of any given historical period than are the laws that follow.

In view of these differences, we may best see in these laws two expressions of God's expectations for his people. The Decalogue is a short summary of the terms of the covenant, intended for permanent use by the community across the generations, as a reminder of its fundamental obligations in obeying the Word of God. The Book of the Covenant is a collection of laws illustrating how the community sought to meet God's expectations at a given stage in its history.

Note that this is not to say that one of these is "really" the Word of God and the other is not. Both are presented as given by Yahweh at Sinai. It is as much Yahweh's expectation that his people obey him in the concrete realities of life at each moment as that they should know in broad outline the abiding concerns which he has for them. Indeed, both kinds of law find their way into the Scriptures: the one, because it has permanent validity as long as the covenant itself endures; the other, because it provides a useful example to later generations, who must similarly find ways to bring all of life under the lordship of God, even in very different circumstances.

When Moses has told the people "all the words of the LORD and all the ordinances," they give the unanimous response, "All the words which the LORD has spoken we will do" (v. 3). This is virtually the same response that they gave when the covenant was first announced (19:8), but now it is given with full awareness of the responsibilities of life in the covenant. They will give this same response yet once more as part of the actual covenant-making ceremony (v. 7); that third expression of commitment will be accepted as confirming the covenant from the side of the people.

The ceremony itself is not only verbal, but concrete and visual. Moses first writes all the words of Yahweh. Then he rises early in the morning (a mark of prompt and eager obedience), builds an altar at the foot of the mountain, and sets up twelve pillars. Burnt offerings and peace offerings of oxen are then made; since no priesthood has yet been appointed, Moses sends young men of the community to carry this out. Moses then performs the three central acts of the ceremony. These acts are singled out by a threefold use of the verb "took" (vv. 6-8). First he *took* the blood from the sacrifices and, reserving half of it in basins, threw the other half against the altar. Second, he *took* the book of the covenant and read it to the people, after which they responded as we have noted. And third, he *took* the remaining blood and threw it on the people.

No detailed explanation is given of the various elements and acts of the ceremony, but the general significance seems clear. The altar represents Yahweh and the pillars the twelve tribes of Israel—the two parties to the covenant. The sacrifices are a solemn act of worship, and the dividing of the blood into two portions, which are then used as described, places the relationship being established into that solemn setting. The reading of the book and the answer of the people indicate that this covenant is no partnership between equals, but one which is given by Yahweh and received by Israel. Moses' concluding words are consistent with this understanding: "Behold the blood of the covenant which the LORD has made with you in accordance with all these words" (v. 8).

3. The instructions carried out (24:9-18).

The rest of the chapter describes the carrying out of the instructions given in the first two verses. While the people remain where they are, Moses goes further up the mountain, accompanied by Aaron, his two sons, and seventy of the elders of Israel. Coming as it does after the covenant-making ceremony, this approach takes on the character of a solemn audience: Yahweh receives the representatives of the nation with which he has just entered into covenant. Thus it provides a confirmation by Yahweh of that covenant.

The extraordinary nature of this audience is indicated in the simple (but unusual) phrase, "And they saw the God of Israel" (v. 10). The frequently expressed biblical warning is that God's holiness is so great that human beings cannot look on him and live. Even after the arrival at Mount Sinai, Moses was told to warn the people, "lest they break through to the LORD to gaze and many of them perish" (19:21). So it is with a sense of wonder that this passage says, "And he did not lay his hand on the chief men of the people of Israel" (v. 11). The point is not that Yahweh has changed, but that his relationship with Israel has changed; he is now the God of Israel, who permits Israel's representatives into his presence. They even participate there in a covenant meal.

This does not mean, however, that divine holiness is aban

doned. Although the representatives see God, there is no attempt to describe him as though he could be viewed with human sight. Only what is under his feet is pictured, and that in a
rather indirect way ("as it were . . . like," v. 10). And, as we see
near the end of this passage (vv. 15-18), Yahweh's glory continues to dwell on Mount Sinai in an awesome way.

Moses, as we were led to expect in the earlier instructions, is
now summoned to continue further up the mountain alone.
There he is to wait to receive something from Yahweh. Just
what he is to receive is left uncertain in the original, but is
probably best understood as including the stone tablets with
the law written by Yahweh, and also further oral instruction.
The inclusion of the latter seems implied both by the length of
time (40 days and nights) that Moses then spends on the
mountain and by the contents of the following chapters. So
Moses goes up the mountain, accompanied by his servant
Joshua (who is only mentioned in passing). He orders the elders to wait, and tells them that Aaron and Hur are to act in
his absence to settle disputes. He then approaches the cloud
and, after a six-day period of waiting, the glory of Yahweh
(which has been covered by the cloud) appears like a de-
vouring fire on the top of the mountain in the sight of the people. Yahweh calls to Moses, who then enters the cloud.

4. Directions for the tabernacle (25:1—31:18).

What follows is to be taken as addressed by Yahweh to
Moses during the 40 days and nights he spent in the cloud on
Mount Sinai. It is separated from the laws of Exodus 20-23 because it serves a different function. Those laws set forth the
responsibilities of life under the covenant, and so they are
presented *before* the covenant is confirmed. The directions for
the tabernacle are given *after* the covenant-making ceremony
and identify the means by which Yahweh will be present with
his people.

That the tabernacle serves this purpose is indicated by what is said about the "glory" of Yahweh before and after the passages concerning the tabernacle. His glory is the manifestation of his presence, often marked (as we have seen) by a cloud or by fire. Just before the instructions for the tabernacle are given, we read that "The glory of the LORD settled on Mount Sinai, and the cloud covered it . . ." (24:16). Immediately after the tabernacle is completed, it is said that "Then the cloud covered the tent of meeting, and the glory of the LORD filled the tabernacle" (40:34). When we add to these references the fact that the Hebrew word for "tabernacle" is from a root meaning "to dwell," it is evident that Yahweh appoints the tabernacle as a suitable way of maintaining his presence with his people as they leave Mount Sinai to continue their journey through the wilderness.

The tabernacle itself, its furnishings, and its service are described in great detail. We might expect that these descriptions would serve as instructions for the workmen who would make the things described. In fact, however, the chapters are not sufficiently clear or complete to serve such a purpose. But even if they had been used in that way, it is difficult to see why they would be preserved, once they had served their purpose, and why they would be included in a book that has become part of the Bible.

It is more likely that the many features described at such length in these chapters all had some symbolic value related to the purpose of the tabernacle. In some instances, we can even make a convincing argument as to what that symbolic value might be. On the whole, however, such an interpretation would constitute a formidable task, with results that would be uneven in their credibility and of doubtful practical use. It seems wiser, therefore, simply to note the main features described.

The instructions begin (25:1-9) with what must be the first step in any building program: arrangements for the gifts that will be needed. So Moses is told, "Speak to the people of Israel, that they take for me an offering; from every man whose heart

makes him willing you shall receive the offering for me"
(v. 2). The tabernacle is ordained by Yahweh; the instructions
are communicated by Moses; and the services will be con-
ducted by the priests. But the tabernacle is intended for the
benefit of all the people, and will be built with their freewill
offerings.

The first item to be described (25:10-22) is the ark, no doubt
because it will be the focal point of Yahweh's presence among
his people. Into this small box, designed to be carried on poles
slipped through rings at its side, will be placed the "testimony"—presumably the tables of stone which Moses will receive
from Yahweh. The ark will have a cover serving to make it
Yahweh's throne, and two winged figures will stand one on
either end of this cover.

The second item (25:23-30) is the table for the bread of the
presence. Like the ark, it will be richly overlaid with gold.
The practice of placing bread before the deity probably origi-
nated in a primitive notion that the deity requires food from
the worshipers. But this notion is not to be found in the Old
Testament, and the bread placed on this table is to be given to
the priests to eat. After this (25:31-40) is described the golden
lampstand with seven branches, the *menorah*. Note that it is a
stand for lamps, and not for candles, which were a much later,
Roman invention.

Next (26:1-36) comes the tabernacle itself, which will contain these articles. Although elaborate in design and richly
ornamented, it is conceived as a portable sanctuary. A veil will
divide it into two parts, the "holy place" and the "most holy
place," and the ark of the covenant will be placed in the latter.
Moses is said (v. 30) not only to receive verbal instructions but
to be shown a plan for the tabernacle while he is on the
mountain.

The altar (27:1-8) will not stand in the tabernacle, of course,
but outside it in a court for which instructions follow
(27:9-19). Although the altar will be made of acacia wood, it is
intended for burnt offerings. Perhaps it is best envisioned as a

framework of boards, the hollow interior of which could be filled with earth or stones as needed. This would be portable, and also meet the requirements of 20:24-25.

The lampstand was described earlier, but instructions for its use are given next (27:20-21), because it is made the responsibility of Aaron and his sons. Thus these verses lead into the next two chapters, which are concerned with the appointment of this family to serve Yahweh as priests. First the priestly garments are described (Exod. 28), and then the ceremony by which they will be consecrated (Exod. 29). The details of these matters need not concern us here.

Two items of furniture remain to be described: the incense altar (30:1-10), which will stand inside the tabernacle; and the bronze laver (30:17-21), which will stand outside it in the court. We might have expected these to be described with the other furnishings, but the descriptions may have been placed here because they also include instructions for the way in which these items will be used by the priests.

Between these last two passages is a paragraph dealing with the half-shekel offering (30:11-16). The occasion for the offering is the taking of a census. For reasons which are not explained, census-taking risks arousing the wrath of Yahweh. In order to avoid that wrath, every adult numbered in the census is to offer a half-shekel as an atonement. More to the point of the context is the fact that this money is to be used to support the service of the tabernacle.

The rest of the chapter is taken up with instructions for the sacred anointing oil (30:22-23) and the incense (30:34-38). Both of these are to be made from the finest ingredients, and used only for the purposes for which they are specifically intended: anointing the objects and persons set aside for Yahweh's service; and burning on the altar of incense within the tabernacle.

The temples of the ancient Near East are sometimes said, in the mythologies, to have been miraculously built by the gods. It is significant, then, that the Bible attributes the construction of the tabernacle and all its fittings to human beings (31:1-11). Indeed, the two chief craftsmen are identified by name and lineage, and are said to be assisted by other able men. The instructions come from Yahweh, as do the skills needed to fulfill them. But the work is done by human beings using natural means.

The last paragraph of this section (31:12-17) is a rather full statement of the law concerning the keeping of the sabbath. Perhaps the specific reason for its inclusion here is to serve as a reminder that work even on the tabernacle and items associated with it must cease on the sabbath. But more generally, its inclusion serves to associate the holy place with the holy day as central to Israel's worship.

Needless to say, there is much in these instructions belonging to a long-gone world which is strange to us. Certainly it is not to be thought that they provide a pattern to be copied by God's people in other times and places. The Book of Exodus does not suggest that such a structure, with its furnishings and personnel, can monopolize or guarantee Yahweh's presence. What it does is to provide for the possibility of his presence in a setting appropriate to the world of biblical times.

Nevertheless, there are points made in these chapters that carry continuing significance. First and foremost, they testify to the indispensable place of worship in the life of the people of God. Those who have been delivered by God's grace, brought into covenant with him, and established as a distinctive community obedient to his Word, are offered his continuing presence in their midst. It is taken for granted that they will acknowledge and celebrate his presence and praise him in appropriate ways.

Second, these chapters bear witness to a God who is among his people, not just as some sort of "spiritual" presence, but by means of concrete, physical things. Ark, table, lamp, altar, oil, building, vestments, priests—it is not that these must be duplicated in every age. But without their equivalents, the awareness of God's presence evaporates and disappears.

Finally, these chapters testify that all matters connected with worship are far too important to the life of God's people to be left to chance, or to the whims of human fad and fancy. However much the externals of worship may vary, they are to be arranged in such a way that the controlling consideration is the Word of the One whose presence they mark and honor.

The concluding verse (31:18) implies that Moses' 40 days and 40 nights on the mountain have now come to an end, and he is now about to return to his people. He is given the tables of stone which had been promised in 24:12; they are here called "the two tables of the testimony" and are said to be "written with the finger of God." Before describing his return, however, the Book of Exodus reports on events that were taking place while Moses was still on the mountain.

5. Israel violates the covenant (32:1-10).

The people have been waiting for Moses to return. The 40 days and 40 nights of his absence are perceived by them as a "delay," and so they devise a scheme of their own. They approach Aaron, who has been left in charge by Moses. Their words to him are abrupt and peremptory: "Up, make us gods, who shall go before us; as for this Moses, the man who brought us up out of the land of Egypt, we do not know what has become of him" (v. 1). At this point, it is not clear whether these "gods, who shall go before us," are to be a substitute for Moses or for Yahweh.

Aaron, surprisingly, raises no objection but proceeds to do as the people request. He collects all of the golden earrings worn by the people, and fashions a calf—a young bull—familiar as an image of deity in the ancient Near East. It seems likely that he does not consider it to be a substitute for Yahweh or even an image of him, but a symbol of the divine presence, comparable to the winged creatures which Moses has just been told are to stand on either side of the ark (25:19-20).

That the people do not see the matter in this light is appar-

ent from the words with which they greet the image: "These
are your gods, O Israel, who brought you out of the land of
Egypt!" (v. 4). Aaron responds by attempting to redirect their
attention to the true Source of their deliverance. He builds an
altar before the image and proclaims, "Tomorrow shall be a
feast to the LORD"—that is, Yahweh (v. 5). The people do not
say anything to the contrary, but their actions the next day are
a resounding contradiction. Their frantic activity, portrayed
in a whole series of verbs ("rose up . . . offered . . . brought . . .
sat down . . . rose up"), culminates in some sort of orgiastic
rites ("play") utterly at odds with the character of the covenant God (v. 6).

The people who have heard the voice of Yahweh,
who have been instructed in the obligations of the covenant,
and who have three times eagerly promised, "All that the
LORD has spoken we will do." Now, even before the covenant
is well under way, they violate it. Their disobedience takes the
form, not of a turning away from religion, but of intense involvement in it. It is, however, a religion perverted by the desire for a god who can be grasped and managed, and that is
worse than no religion at all.

The scene then shifts from the foot of the mountain to the
top, from which Moses is about to return. He is informed by
Yahweh about what has been taking place below. In addition
to describing the people's actions, Yahweh expresses his anger.
He does this at first indirectly; he tells Moses, "Go down; for
your people, whom you brought up out of the land of Egypt,
have corrupted themselves" (v. 7). Thus Yahweh dissociates
himself from Israel (rather like one parent saying to the other,
"*Your* children have certainly misbehaved today") and leaves
the responsibility with Moses. He also expresses his anger
directly, saying to Moses: "I have seen this people, and behold,
it is a stiff-necked people; now therefore let me alone, that my
wrath may burn hot against them and I may consume them"
(v. 9). He concludes by making Moses a proposition: "but of
you I will make a great nation" (v. 9). The promise taken from

Israel Yahweh offers to transfer to Moses and his descendants.

We are likely to be troubled by passages like this which refer to the *wrath* of God. Language like this testifies, however, to the personal quality of God's relationship to his people. He is not like some distant tyrant who hands down arbitrary decrees to his subjects and then flies into a rage if his decrees are violated. He is, rather, like a parent who gives the children instructions that are in their own best interest. When the children rebel and disobey, a parent is of course deeply hurt and offended, even angry. It may be that a parent's first reaction, at such a time, is to throw his or her hands up and disclaim all further responsibility. But the anger is an expression of love, and love does not let go that easily. So it is, as we shall see, with God's love for his people.

The Covenant Renewed

1. Intercession, repentance and forgiveness (32:11—33:17).

Moses' first intercession

When Moses hears what the people have done, he takes their part before Yahweh. When he has previously spoken to Yahweh concerning Israel, it has been to convey Israel's response to the divine word (see, for example, 19:8-9). Now Moses goes further; he speaks to Yahweh, not simply to report but to intercede. He picks up on a hint that Yahweh himself dropped when he said, "let me alone, that my wrath may burn . . ." Moses does not let Yahweh alone, but seeks to turn aside his wrath.

He does so by giving three reasons why Yahweh should not destroy Israel. (1) They are in fact his people, despite his effort to dissociate himself from them, because he has delivered them. Note the gentle contradiction in Moses' words: "O LORD, why does thy wrath burn hot against *thy* people, whom *thou* hast brought forth out of the land of Egypt?" (32:11). (2) His honor is at stake: "Why should the Egyptians say, 'With evil intent did he bring them forth, to slay them in the mountains, and to consume them from the face of the earth'?" (32:12). (3) He committed himself by his unconditional promise to the patriarchs, Israel's ancestors: "Remember Abraham, Isaac, and Israel, thy servants, to whom thou didst swear by thine own self, and didst say to them, 'I will multiply your descendants as the stars of heaven, and all this land that I have promised I will give to your descendants, and they shall inherit it for ever' " (32:13). Note that, by saying this, Moses has implicitly refused to take personal advantage of Yahweh's wrath by accepting the proposition for the transfer of the promise to himself and his descendants.

As a result of Moses' intercession, "the LORD repented of the evil which he thought to do to his people" (32:14). Readers are likely to find this a rather troublesome verse. This is in part because the way the words are translated is open to misunderstanding. "Evil" here does not have a moral connotation. What Yahweh "thought to do to his people" is perfectly just—a consequence of their faithlessness and disobedience. It can be called "evil" only in the sense that it would have been experienced by Israel as an unimaginably painful thing. To say that Yahweh "repented" of it is simply to say that he changed his mind.

Of course, the very idea of a God who changes his mind is a challenge to some of our conventional notions about deity. Yet the Bible frequently pictures Yahweh doing just that, often as a result of the prayers of his people or the intercessions of his prophets. This is not to say that he is fickle. Indeed, Moses' intercession is a plea that Yahweh will be faithful to his prior deeds and promises; Moses is praying, in effect, "thy will be done." But Yahweh is a sovereign God, not enslaved by a list of attributes. He enters into dialogue with his people. He is free to respond as he will in this dialogue. Even at the expense of consistency, his justice is tempered with mercy.

Moses returns to the people

After his successful intercession, Moses goes down the mountain, bearing "the two tables of the testimony." He is again accompanied by Joshua, who has been with him on the mountain. As they draw near, they hear shouts, and Joshua jumps to the conclusion that a battle is in progress (not a very surprising idea on his part, since he is the leader of Israel's army). But Moses has sharper ears; he declares it to be the sound of singing.

When Moses comes near enough to see the calf and the dancing, he reacts in a way we do not expect. Despite the opening words of his intercession, "O LORD, why does thy wrath burn hot against thy people?", we now read that "Moses' anger burned hot" (32:19). But this is consistent with the office he holds. When Moses is with Yahweh on the mountain, he represents Israel. He identifies with the people and intercedes for them when they are sinful. When he returns to Israel at the foot of the mountain, he represents Yahweh. He expresses the divine wrath and condemnation of Israel's sin, forcing the people to face the enormity of their idolatry. So, in a burst of activity that must have brought the revels to a sudden halt, Moses burns the calf (is it, perhaps, a wooden image plated with gold?), grinds to powder what remains, scatters it on the water, and makes the people drink it. There could be no more effective demonstration of the impotence of this "god" which they have preferred to Yahweh!

Moses then turns to Aaron, who was left with responsibility for the people. "What did this people do to you," he asks, "that you have brought a great sin upon them?" (32:21). The question is ambiguous. It means either "What did they do to compel you to do what they wanted?" or "What did they do to deserve such treatment from you?" But there is no ambiguity about Aaron's reply. He tries to minimize his own role and put all of the blame on the people. He begins with an echo of Moses' words to Yahweh: "Let not the anger of my lord burn hot" (32:22). The irony is, however, that when Moses spoke like that, he was interceding for Israel, while Aaron is blaming Israel and making excuses for himself. And he ends with the lame assertion that he simply threw the gold into the fire, "and

there came out this calf" (32:24). Aaron has been at Moses'
side in the key events of the exodus, and has been serving as
Moses' deputy. But he has used his high office to sanction the
people's idolatry, spreading the cloak of his authority over
their disobedience to the word of God. Now he seeks to avoid
taking responsibility for what he has done. His inferiority to
Moses is striking.

Moses' initial actions were a declaration of the people's guilt
in having made and worshiped an image. There is still to be
judgment, though Moses' intercession has turned aside total
destruction. He calls for a muster of all those faithful to
Yahweh. Only members of his own tribe, Levi, respond.
Moses then commands them, in Yahweh's name, to carry out
a mass execution among the unfaithful of Israel. There is no
denying the harshness of the judgment, but no joy is expressed
over the slaughter. Rather, emphasis is placed on the high cost
at which the Levites have become a special class of Yahweh's
servants among his people. Again we find underscored the unconditional character of Yahweh's demand for loyalty, the se-
riousness of Israel's lack of faith, and the dire consequences of
turning to gods devised by the worshipers themselves.

Moses' second intercession

The next day, Moses announces his intention to approach
Yahweh, in the hope of atoning for the people's sin. The question of how this second intercession is to be understood in relation to the first is difficult. It is possible that Moses' first
intercession should be seen as having resulted in Yahweh's
changing his mind about the *total* destruction of Israel, though
there would still be punishment for Israel's sin. Severe punishment has in fact been meted out by the Levites. Now Moses'
second intercession may be intended to seek the forgiveness
that will mean an end to the punishment.

More likely, however, we are not to take the chapter as a
mere report of a sequence of events. We saw, in regard to
Exodus 19, how the repeated movement of Moses up and

down the mountain makes sense as a statement of his office. Here, too, the alternation between Moses as intercessor and Moses as spokesman and agent of Yahweh serves a similar purpose.

In this second intercession, Moses fully acknowledges Israel's guilt: "Alas, this people have sinned a great sin" (32:31). He also fully identifies with his people: if Yahweh will not forgive them, "blot me, I pray thee, out of thy book which thou hast written" (32:32). Yahweh responds by asserting his freedom to grant petitions or to deny them, according to his sovereign will. First, he will blot only sinners out of his book. Second, Moses is to lead the people on to the promised land, and Yahweh's angel will go before them; the covenant is still intact. Finally, there will be further punishment in the future. The closing verse of the chapter is a kind of footnote to that third point. It reports that the further punishment came in the form of a plague, though it does not say when or where it took place.

The opening verses of Exodus 33 are an elaboration of Yahweh's words to Moses in 32:34. He will lead Israel to the promised land; the angel of Yahweh will go with them; those who stand in the way will be driven out. But now we are told for the first time that this "angel" who will accompany them represents less than the full presence of Yahweh. "But I will not go up among you," he says, "lest I consume you in the way, for you are a stiff-necked people" (33:3). Since the tabernacle was to be the dwelling-place of Yahweh in the midst of his people, this statement in effect cancels out the orders for its construction. Israel is to set out for Canaan, protected by Yahweh but deprived of the glory which they experienced at Sinai.

The people's repentance

The people respond to this announcement with sorrow and, as an expression of their sincere remorse, they divest themselves of all ornaments. The report of this is followed by a paragraph (33:7-11) which appears at first to have little to do with the context. It concerns something called a "tent of meeting," though it is clearly not the same "tent of meeting" referred to in connection with the tabernacle (which has, of course, not been built). Rather, it is described as a tent pitched at some distance from Israel's camp, to which people could go with matters they wanted to put before Yahweh. There Moses would go, and Yahweh would speak with him, his presence marked by the pillar of cloud. The connection with the context lies in part in the contrast between the presence of Yahweh as it might have been if the tabernacle had been built, and his presence as it is in the wake of Israel's sin. There is also a connection in that the people, who have already shown their repentance by removing their ornaments, now show great reverence even before the rather limited evidences of Yahweh's presence. When Moses goes to the tent, the people stand at their doors, and remain there to worship when the pillar of cloud descends.

Moses' third intercession

These signs of a new attitude on the part of Israel form the backdrop for a third intercession by Moses. What he seeks is another change of mind on Yahweh's part, this time about the word that Yahweh will not go up among the people of Israel. He appeals to what Yahweh has spoken to him personally; he appeals also to the covenant: "Consider too that this nation is thy people" (33:13).

Moses readily gains Yahweh's assent: "My presence will go with you, and I will give you rest" (33:14). So quickly is the assent given, that it seems as if Moses has some appeals left over. They are not needed, but he delivers them anyway. In fact, however, his further words provide a commentary on the vital importance of what he is seeking. "If thy presence will not go with me," he says, "do not carry us up from here" (33:15).

Without it, there is no reason for the community to go on. Nothing can take its place, Numbers, security, wealth, or influence are no indication that God is pleased with his people. Only his presence provides that: "For how shall it be known that I have found favor in thy sight, I and thy people? Is it not in thy going with us, so that we are distinct, I and thy people, from all other people that are upon the face of the earth?" (33:16).

Moses' intercession, then, is successful. "This very thing that you have spoken I will do," Yahweh tells him (33:17). The door is open for the covenant to be renewed.

2. Yahweh's glory (33:18—34:9).

Moses next asks to be shown Yahweh's glory. Given the connection between "glory" and divine presence (see, for example, 24:15-18), this seems to constitute a request for a confirmation of the favor Yahweh has just granted. Both the request and Yahweh's reply are reminiscent of the dialogue in Exodus 3, when Moses asked for the divine name. Now the reply consitutes a lesson in what human beings may see of the divine glory. Yahweh will reveal his goodness, his name, his grace, and his mercy; but he will preserve his sovereign freedom: "I will make all my goodness pass before you, and will proclaim before you my name 'The LORD'; and I will be gracious to whom I will be gracious, and will show mercy on whom I will show mercy" (33:19).

But there is a limit to what any person—even Moses—can experience of God. "You cannot see my face; for man shall not see me and live" (33:20). To know God directly, as one knows a fellow human being, is beyond human capacity. So great is his glory that only he can protect those who come in contact with it. This is put in bold and picturesque language in the words Yahweh speaks to Moses: "Behold, there is a place by me where you shall stand upon the rock; and while my glory passes by I will put you in a cleft of the rock, and I will cover you with my hand until I have passed by; then I will take away my hand, and you shall see my back; but my face shall not be seen" (33:21-23).

This dialogue presumably takes place in the tent of meeting, because at the beginning of Exodus 34, Moses is told to present himself the next morning on the top of Mount Sinai. There Yahweh will appear to him as promised. First, however, Moses is to prepare two tables of stone, like the ones which were broken, and bring those with him so that Yahweh may write the same words on them. In this way, Moses' request to see Yahweh's glory, and the fulfillment of that request, are made more than just a matter of Moses' own personal satisfaction. He is granted the vision by virtue of his office. This is underlined by Moses' response when, as promised, "The LORD passed before him" (34:6). He does not stand indulging in some private ecstacy. He bows his head and worships, of course; but as he does so he renews his prayer for Yahweh's presence in the midst of his people, his forgiveness of them, and his continuing relationship with them.

The vision itself is given in solemn words, with that combination of sternness tempered with compassion which we have noted before: "The LORD passed before him, and proclaimed, 'The LORD, the LORD, a God merciful and gracious, slow to anger, and abounding in steadfast love and faithfulness, keeping steadfast love for thousands, forgiving iniquity and transgression and sin, but who will by no means clear the guilty, visiting the iniquity of the fathers upon the children and the children's children, to the third and the fourth generation' " (34:6-7).

3. Renewal of the covenant (34:10-35).

Next comes the anticipated renewal of the covenant. It begins with Yahweh's announcement, "Behold, I make a covenant" (v. 10). It continues with a promise which provides reassurance for a people about to continue a perilous journey; Yahweh will be at work with Israel in a new and startling way that will be a witness to surrounding nations. Then a series of commands is given. They seem to function in the same way as did the Decalogue and the Book of the Covenant when the covenant was originally made. They contain, in fact, laws identical with or similar to those in that earlier section of legal material, though the ones given here are concerned primarily with worship. Probably we are to understand these as recorded here by way of reminder, representing the whole body of covenant obligations. It may be that they have to do with worship because they follow in the wake of Israel's idolatry in worshiping the golden calf. Certainly the initial command is appropriate in this context; it forbids Israel "to make a covenant with the inhabitants of the land whither you go" (v. 12), because that would involve participation in their worship of other gods.

The verses which conclude these commands are rather ambiguous. Yahweh tells Moses to write these words, which are the basis of the covenant. Then we are told that "he wrote upon the tables the words of the covenant, the ten commandments" (v. 28). Is this "he" Moses or Yahweh? Probably, in view of the promise in 34:1, we are to understand that it is Yahweh. If so, what is it that Moses is to write: all of the covenant obligations, or only those which have been reiterated or added here? Probably, in view of 24:4, 7, we are to understand that this new document is to be merely a supplement, since the previous one is presumably still in existence.

To attempt to harmonize all the details, however, may result in missing the main point. The author is here bringing together older material (for example, a little collection of laws having to do with worship) into a broader framework that teaches about the relationship between Yahweh and his people. Yahweh had chosen and delivered Israel, and had then set forth his Word for them, as they became his covenant people. They had eagerly assented, and he had solemnly made covenant with them. Then, at the very time when he was making provision to dwell in their midst, they were grossly unfaithful to him. The covenant had been broken before it was even well begun, and Israel stood under judgment. But the people repented and mended their ways, Moses interceded for them, and Yahweh had mercy. So now, in a kind of abbreviated replay of the previous occasion, Yahweh renews the covenant.

From the outset, the covenant was an expression of God's grace to an utterly helpless and undeserving people. If that point could somehow have been missed before, it can surely not be avoided here. The covenant is renewed because—and *only* because—God forgives and accepts sinners. His grace sustains the relationship in the face of repeated human unfaithfulness.

The final paragraph of the chapter returns to the subject of Moses as spokesman of Yahweh. Coming down the mountain, bearing the tables of the testimony, he is unaware that rays of light are shining from his face, as a result of his having been talking with Yahweh. But Aaron and all the people are afraid to approach him because of this glow. Only after he calls them do Aaron and the leaders come near and, after he has spoken to them, the rest of the people as well. He then tells them the commandments he has received from Yahweh.

When Moses has finished speaking, he places a veil over his face. He does not wear it, as we might expect, in order to spare the Israelites the sight of his shining face, of which they were at first so afraid. For he removes the veil, not only when he enters the tent of meeting to speak with Yahweh, but also when he comes out and tells the people what is commanded. Thus he apparently wears the veil only when he is not functioning as Yahweh's spokesman.

The rays of light from Moses' face indicate the closeness of his association with Yahweh; he reflects something of the divine radiance, and this sets him apart from the rest of the people of Israel. The veil, on the other hand, indicates that it is only by virtue of his office that he is set apart in this way;

when he is not exercising that office, he is among his fellow-Israelites with the radiance not seen.

This is an appropriate place at which to summarize what is said in the Book of Exodus about Moses' role. He is portrayed as a great man, not only in his own generation but in the whole history of Israel. If the book has a hero (other than Yahweh himself), that hero is surely Moses.

Yet Moses is not depicted as superhuman in his virtues. Although his heroic qualities are drawn in bold strokes, his humanity and weakness are not concealed. We see him resisting his call, not once but over and over; and his lack of trust in Yahweh, especially in the early part of his ministry, is remarkable.

The fact is that Moses' greatness does not derive from his person or attainments, but from his office—and his office comes from Yahweh alone. His ministry is many-faceted. He is Yahweh's agent: performing signs before Pharaoh, leading the people out of Egypt, empowering them to win victory over their enemies, and implementing both judgment and blessing. He is Yahweh's spokesman: announcing his word to Pharaoh and the Egyptians, but even more to the people of Israel, and reporting this response. He is the intercessor when Israel sins. He is the priest at the covenant-making ceremony. He is the judge who settles disputes among them. We may sum up these varied roles by saying that, in the Book of Exodus, Moses is the mediator of the covenant.

As covenant mediator, Moses is unique: "the LORD used to speak to Moses face to face, as a man speaks to his friend" (33:11). No other person in the Old Testament is called to a ministry just like his. His descendants do not follow him as leaders of Israel, and there is no "Mosaic office" in later times. Strictly speaking, Moses has no successor.[1]

[1]In the New Testament, Jesus' ministry is comparable to, although it far surpasses, that of Moses. It is noteworthy that, in Matthew's gospel, Jesus is deliberately presented as the new and greater Moses: his life is threatened by a wicked king, he comes out of Egypt, he announces God's Word from a mountain, etc.

On the other hand, in the Book of Exodus Moses embodies the various ministries carried out in later Israel. He is depicted as the greatest of Israel's prophets; the story of his call follows the same pattern as those of Isaiah (Isa. 6) and Jeremiah (Jer. 1). To speak for Yahweh is, of course, the chief role of a prophet. Although less commonly recognized, to be agent of Yahweh and intercessor on behalf of Israel are also part of the prophet's calling.[2] Thus the prophetic office is rooted in Moses' ministry.

The portrayals of Moses as priest and judge of Israel are less developed. It is Aaron, not Moses, who is designated as the ancestor of Israel's priesthood. But Aaron has no independent place of his own. His task is to assist Moses, serving as his deputy; but the initiative and responsibility lie with Moses. So also with the judges who are appointed at Jethro's suggestion: "they judged the people at all times; hard cases they brought to Moses, but any small matter they decided themselves" (18:26). Ultimately, the priestly and judicial offices are also rooted in Moses' ministry.

Thus the varied ministries in later Israel have their source in Moses' role as covenant mediator. He was appointed to his office by Yahweh, that through him Israel would be delivered from bondage and joined to Yahweh in an abiding relationship. All derivative ministries exist to serve the continuing activity of Yahweh the deliverer and covenant God.

4. Construction of the tabernacle (35:1—40:38).

This section is virtually identical to that containing the instructions for the tabernacle (25:1—31:18). There are some omissions, abridgments, expansions, and rearrangements. These are relatively minor, and in some cases can be explained

---

[2]The prophets do not just communicate ideas, but serve as agents to accomplish the purposes of the God whose word they proclaim; this can be seen most clearly in the "signs" they perform (for example, Jer. 19 and Ezek. 4). A good example of the prophet as intercessor is seen in Amos 7:1-6.

as providing a more logical order. It is not necessary, for our purposes, to reexamine this material.

There is, however, a question that needs to be considered. Why is such a large block of material repeated in all of its overwhelming detail? If the intention were simply to communicate historical information, it would be sufficient to say, simply, "Moses and the people of Israel constructed the tabernacle and its funishings according to Yahweh's instructions."

But the intention goes beyond mere reporting, and has to do with the character of the relationship between Yahweh and his people. Yahweh was present with Israel at Mount Sinai. There he made a covenant with them and there they pledged themselves to obey him. The instructions of 25:1—31:18 were given by Yahweh to provide for his continuing presence with his people as they set out to journey through the wilderness. But without even waiting for Moses to announce these instructions, the people make their own arrangements for a golden calf to go with them. For breaking the covenant in this way, Israel is threatened with judgment and even annihilation. But their repentance, coupled with Moses' intercessions, lead to forgiveness and covenant renewal. This means another opportunity for obedience. The obedience takes the form of constructing the tabernacle which was previously commanded. To emphasize the unqualified obedience of the people, forgiven and restored to the covenant, the Book of Exodus uses this literary device of detailed repetition.

This lends great significance to the concluding paragraph of this section (and of the entire book). The command to Moses, before the episode of the golden calf, was "And let them make me a sanctuary, that I may dwell in their midst" (25:8). The promise included in this command was reiterated in the midst of the instructions for the tabernacle: "And I will dwell among the people of Israel, and will be their God. And they shall know that I am the LORD their God, who brought them forth out of the land of Egypt that I might dwell among them" (29:45-46). Israel had known that presence in the pillar of cloud and fire that accompanied them to Sinai. At Mount Sinai, the cloud covered the mountain and the glory of Yahweh was revealed from within the cloud. Now, after the tabernacle has finally been completed, we read that "the cloud covered the tent of meeting" (again viewed as part of the tabernacle) "and the glory of the LORD filled the tabernacle" (40:34).

Thus the concluding paragraph looks backward, and sees the presence of Yahweh, known in the past, enshrined now in Israel's midst. But it also looks forward to what is to come. "For throughout all their journeys the cloud of the LORD was upon the tabernacle by day, and fire was in it by night, in the sight of all the house of Israel" (40:38). Yahweh and his people are on their way, together, toward the goal of the promise.

Conclusion

Now that we have worked our way through the 40 chapters of the Book of Exodus, it is time for us to look back to see what can be said in summary.

We noted at the outset that the book is a narrative; that is, it tells a story. The Exodus story has two main parts. In the first, God delivers Israel from bondage. In the second, he makes a covenant with Israel.

The story opens, then, with Israel in slavery. The people called by this name are the heirs of a promise made to their ancestors—a promise of divine blessing. They have, in fact, experienced one portion of that blessing; they have grown in number from a single family to a sizable population. But they live as aliens in the land of Egypt. Their very increase has aroused the oppressive power of the king of Egypt, and so has contributed to the absence of the other portion of the promised blessing; they are not a free and responsible nation. The one without the other is worse than no blessing at all.

Deliverance begins when God enters the picture, at first unobtrusively and then more and more openly. He prepares and appoints a leader, Moses, to be his representative to the Egyptian king and the people of Israel. Moses' initial reluctance is gradually overcome, and the struggle for liberation begins. The contest with Pharaoh is a long one, for he is the representative of all opposition to the will and purpose of

Yahweh the God of Israel. One plague follows another, as Pharaoh resists the challenge to his absolute rule. The outcome is never in doubt, of course; but the struggle is prolonged, so that it may be evident to all that Yahweh is stronger than all opposition and that his victory is overwhelming. When Israel crosses the sea, the victory is complete.

Israel's deliverance means freedom from slavery in Egypt and freedom for a new life in the land of Canaan. The promise of divine blessing is on its way to complete fulfillment. The people are given appropriate observances to commemorate the victory, and Yahweh provides food and water for their immediate needs. But if the contest with Pharaoh is over, that with Israel is not. The people complain and rebel. They must still be fashioned for a future lived in covenant with Yahweh.

The establishing of this covenant is the subject of the second part of the Exodus narrative. Amid the most impressive evidences of Yahweh's presence and power, the assembly receives at Mount Sinai the law which is to guide the life of the community. The content of the law includes both the abiding fundamentals of the divine will and specific applications of that will to the life of the community. The manner of its presentation strikes a balance between the directness of Yahweh's relationship with all of his people and the crucial role of Moses as mediator of that relationship. What is given to Israel is not the burdensome demands of an arbitrary deity but the benevolent instructions of a God who wills that his people live so as to enjoy the fullness of his blessing.

That Israel perceives the law as a good gift is indicated by the cheerful readiness with which it is accepted. The covenant is then solemnly confirmed. In preparation for the continuation of the journey toward the promised land, Yahweh instructs Moses about the tabernacle, in which the divine presence will accompany the people. But before Moses can even announce these arrangements to them, Israel violates the newly-established covenant. The worship of the golden calf is a blatant act of unfaithfulness, and shatters the relationship between the people and their God. Judgment follows, but repentance and intercession are met with forgiveness. The tabernacle is constructed, and the story ends with Yahweh dwelling among his people as the covenant community journeys toward its goal.

The story we have just summarized is good news. It has been told over and over across the centuries, and is still told today, because it is addressed to all generations of God's people. While the narrative relates events of the distant past, it does so in such a way as to proclaim God's grace at work today and every day. He hears the cries of those who are oppressed, helpless, and hopeless. He comes to their aid, not because they are deserving, but because he is faithful to his promises. He provides them with leaders, delivers them from their desperate circumstances, and sets them on the way to the fullness of his blessing. He makes them his people and becomes their God, calling them to a manner of life appropriate to their new condition. He disciplines them when they are unfaithful, but he also forgives them when they are penitent. He does not cast them off, but is with them always.

Those who hear this story find their sense of identity renewed, their faith strengthened, and their spirits aroused to celebration.

Bibliography

Commentaries

Cassuto, Ulrich. *A Commentary on the Book of Exodus.* Jerusalem: Magnes, Hebrew University, 1967.

Childs, Brevard S. *The Book of Exodus: A Critical, Theological Commentary (The Old Testament Library).* Philadelphia: Westminster, 1974.

Clements, R. E. *Exodus (The Cambridge Bible Commentary, New English Bible).* Cambridge: Cambridge University Press, 1972.

Greenberg, Moshe. *Understanding Exodus.* New York: Behrman House, 1969.

Hyatt, J. P. *Commentary on Exodus (New Century Bible).* Greenwood, SC: Attic, 1971.

Noth, Martin. *Exodus: A Commentary (The Old Testament Library).* Philadelphia: Westminster, 1962.

Rylaarsdam, J. Coert. "The Book of Exodus: Introduction and Exegesis." *The Interpreter's Bible,* Vol. I. Edited by George Arthur Buttrick. New York: Abingdon, 1952.

Zenger, Erich. *Das Buch Exodus.* Düsseldorf: Patmos, 1978.

Other

Buttrick, George Arthur, ed. *The Interpreter's Dictionary of the Bible.* 4 vols. New York: Abingdon, 1962 (plus supplementary volume, 1976).

Kaiser, Otto. *Introduction to the Old Testament: A Presentation of its Results and Problems.* Minneapolis: Augsburg, 1975.